Guitar Lesson
VALUE PACK
SEVEN CLASSIC BOOKS, ALL IN ONE
BY JOHN STIX AND YOICHI ARAKAWA

ISBN 978-1-4803-9527-5

HAL•LEONARD®
CORPORATION
7777 W. BLUEMOUND RD. P.O. BOX 13819 MILWAUKEE, WI 53213

In Australia Contact:
Hal Leonard Australia Pty. Ltd.
4 Lentara Court
Cheltenham, Victoria, 3192 Australia
Email: ausadmin@halleonard.com.au

Visit Hal Leonard Online at
www.halleonard.com

INTRODUCTION

In its short history, rock music has produced no band more melodically memorable than The Beatles or more raucous and bombastic than The Who. Coming from seemingly opposite directions, both bands lean on the acoustic guitar for the foundation of their songs. From Stone Temple Pilots to Led Zeppelin and Elvis Presley to Soul Asylum, the acoustic guitar has had a profound impact on the rock music that any generation calls their own. MTV even made a side business out of bringing us the "Unplugged" sounds of electric artists from Nirvana to Eric Clapton.

The electricity of the acoustic guitar existed long before MTV discovered it. You can hear it used in: rock-influenced blues (Jimi Hendrix, "Hear My Train A Comin'," Eddie Van Halen, "Take Your Whiskey Home"), folk music (Jimmy Page, "Black Mountain Side," The Aliman Brothers, "Little Martha"), classical music (Randy Rhoads, "Dee," Yngwie Malmsteen, "Coming Bach"), ethnic music (Robbie Krieger, "Spanish Caravan," Al DiMeola, "Mediterranean Sundance") and country music (Steve Howe, "Clap," George Harrison, "I've Just Seen A Face"). The acoustic guitar has also often been used as a songwriters tool. As it was true for rock composers in the '50s so it is four decades later. Kim Thayil of Soundgarden comments: "Most of our songs are written on bass, acoustic guitar, and frequently, a 12-string acoustic. Even our hardcore songs were written on acoustic guitar. It's just sped up and turned up when we put it on a record."

Acoustic Rock For Guitar will provide you with a user-friendly introduction to some classic strumming and fingerpicking techniques, using various rock songs for reference. Just spend as much time as you need with the Notation Legend, and let's play!

STRUMMING

Most people strum with a pick (Van Halen) or thumb-pick (Johnny Winter), while some people use their thumb (Jeff Beck) or thumb and fingers (Steve Howe). There is no one right way to strum, just a variety of choices. Whether you choose to play with your fingers or with a pick is a personal decision based on the style of music and the sound you want to produce. Even Jimi Hendrix songs have been arranged for fingerstyle guitar!

NOTATION LEGEND

Down and Up Strokes:

This symbol (⊓) indicates a downstroke (strumming toward the ground). This symbol (∨) indicates an upstroke (strumming towards the ceiling).

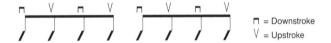

⊓ = Downstroke
∨ = Upstroke

Muting:

When playing open chords, mute or deaden the strings by lightly resting the palm of your strumming hand on the strings. When playing barre chords, you may use this same technique or simply lift your fretting hand slightly off the strings. Hall of Fame rhythm guitarists from Pete Townsend ("Won't Get Fooled Again") to Eddie Van Halen ("Little Guitars") use this technique to great advantage.

✗ = Mute

Accent:

This symbol (>) indicates an accent, which tells you to put more emphasis on a particular place in the music. Accents are a good way to spice up what you're playing.

> = Accent

Hammer-on:

Pick the first (lower) note, then "hammer on" to sound the higher note with another finger by fretting it without picking.

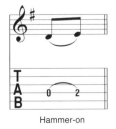

Hammer-on

Pull-off:

Place both fingers on the notes to be sounded. Pick the first (higher) note, then sound the lower note by "pulling off" the finger on the higher note while keeping the lower note fretted.

Pull-off

Bending:

Pick the note and bend up.

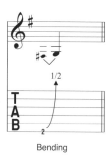

Bending

EXPLAINING TABLATURE

Tablature is a paint-by-number language telling you which notes to play on the fingerboard. Each of the six lines represents a string on the guitar. The numbers on the lines indicate which frets to press down. Note that tablature does not indicate the rhythm.

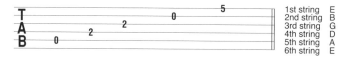

1st string	E
2nd string	B
3rd string	G
4th string	D
5th string	A
6th string	E

PRACTICE TIPS

1. Strive for a steady, fluid strum, alternating between downstrokes and upstrokes. Just as you do when with picking out riffs or solos, your controlled picking technique will define the "feel" of the music.

2. Keep your wrist loose.

3. Pay close attention to accents. They not only give you an edge and help define your style, but they also make strumming more percussive, particularly when combined with muting.

4. Downstrokes and upstrokes placed on the patterns are only suggestions by the authors. They are intended merely as a place to start. This is your music, so play the way you feel most comfortable or the way you want to hear it.

5. The best way to practice smooth and accurate strumming is to play with other musicians, or along with recorded music, a metronome, or a drum machine.

HOW TO READ RHYTHM CHARTS

The rhythm charts presented in the Strumming section observe the basic rules of music notation. The only difference is the use of slashes in place of conventional oval-shaped notes. Below is a brief review of various slash and rest symbols and an explanation of time signature. For greater details, please refer to music theory books.

Rhythm Slashes and Rests

Rhythm slashes tell you the duration of how long the chord being played should sound or sustain. For example, a whole note lasts for four counts or beats per measure, a quarter note for one count, and so on. Likewise, a rest tells you when to stop playing, and for how long. The following chart summarizes various note, slash and rest symbols. Counts or numbers of beats, indicate how many counts each chord should last (or be silent, in the case of rests) during a measure of 4/4.

NAME OF NOTE	NOTATION	RHYTHM SLASHES	REST SYMBOLS	COUNTS OR NUMBER OF BEATS
Whole Note	o	◇	▬	◇ 1 2 3 4
Half Note	♩	◇	▬	◇ ◇ 1 2 3 4
Quarter Note	♩	/	𝄽	/ / / / 1 2 3 4
Eighth Note	♪ ♫	♪ ♫	𝄾	1 & 2 & 3 & 4 &
Sixteenth Note	♪ ♬	♪ ♬	𝄿	1 2 3 4 2 2 3 4 3 2 3 4 4 2 3 4
Eighth-Note Triplet	³	³		³ ³ ³ ³ 1 2 3 2 2 3 3 2 3 4 2 3
*Dotted Quarter Note	♩.	/.	𝄾 𝄽 or 𝄽 𝄾	/. 𝄾 /. 𝄾 1 & 2 3 & 4
*Dotted Eighth Note	♪.	♪.	𝄾.	/. / /. / ♪ 𝄾 ♪ 𝄾 1 2 3 4 2 2 3 4 3 2 3 4 4 2 3 4

*A dot increases a note value by one-half (eg: ♩. = ♩ + ♪ or ♩. = ♩ + ♪)

Time Signatures

The time signature placed at the beginning of a piece of music tells you how to count time. It consists of two numbers, one placed above the other. The upper number tells you the number of beats in one measure. The lower number indicates what kind of note receives one beat, or count. For example, in 4/4, the most common and popular time signature, there are four beats to the measure, and a quarter note receives one beat. Below is a summary of various time signatures.

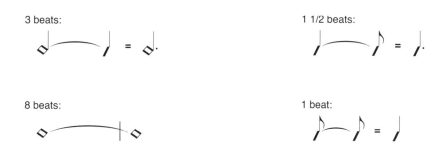

Tie

A tie is a curved line connecting two slashes of the same chord. It is an indication that the chord is to be sounded only once and held for the time value of both slashes combined.

All the songs on Hints Allegations and Things Left Unsaid were started with an acoustic guitar.

—Ed Roland (Collective Soul)

BASIC STRUMMING EXAMPLES

The basic one-bar patterns listed in Exs. 1–75 are only a small portion of the endless possibilities available. Create your own by changing them or by using your imagination and starting from scratch. Remember, you can play any chord you like. For Exs. 1–15, we have given you simple patterns, using mainly quarter notes and eighth notes.

Ex. 1 is used in the Beatles song "Rocky Raccoon." See Ex. 92.

Ex. 3 can be used to play another Beatles classic, "Can't Buy Me Love." See Ex. 76. Reverse Ex. 3 and use all downstrokes to duplicate a strum from Led Zeppelin's "Babe I'm Gonna Leave You." See Ex. 80.

A variation of Ex. 4 can be heard in the opening bar of Rod Stewart's "Maggie May." See Ex. 77.

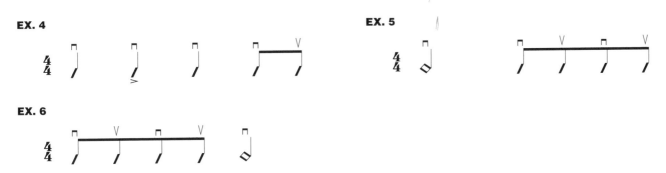

Ex. 7 will get you started playing Guns N' Roses' "Used to Love Her." See Ex. 82.

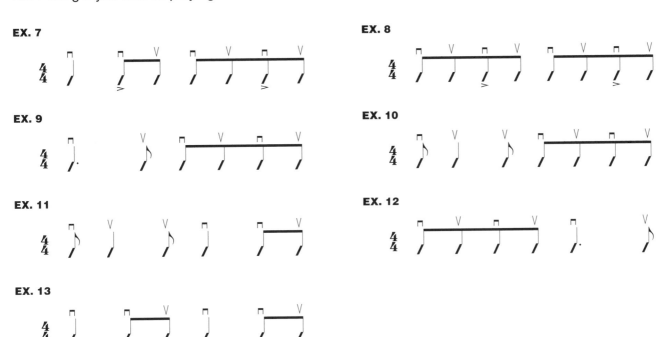

Ex. 14 is used by The Allman Brothers Band in the song "Jessica." See Ex. 93.

EX. 14   **EX. 15**

Exs. 16–21 show off various syncopation patterns. With ties, the accents fall onto the normally weak or unaccented beats (usually upbeats).

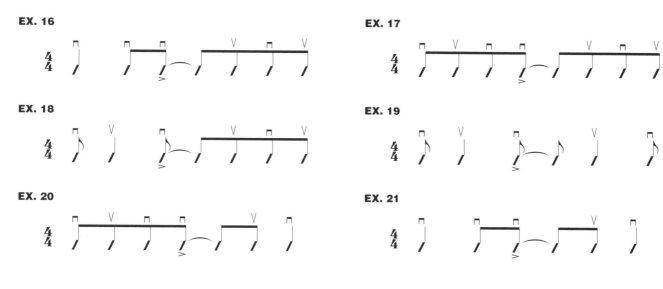

Exs. 22–31 provide you with examples to practice muting.

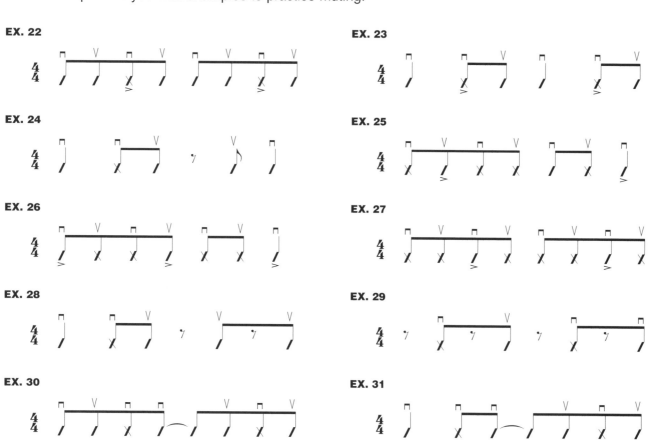

Exs. 32–52 introduce the sixteenth note. Ex. 32 is used to play the outro of James Taylor's "Fire and Rain." See Ex. 99.

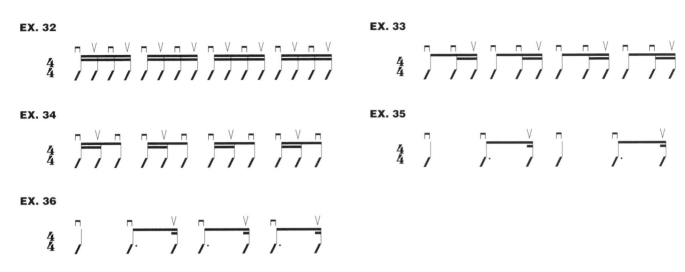

Ex. 37 is used to play "Pinball Wizard" by The Who. See Ex. 97.

Ex. 39 is similar to Mr. Big's "To Be With You." See Ex. 98.

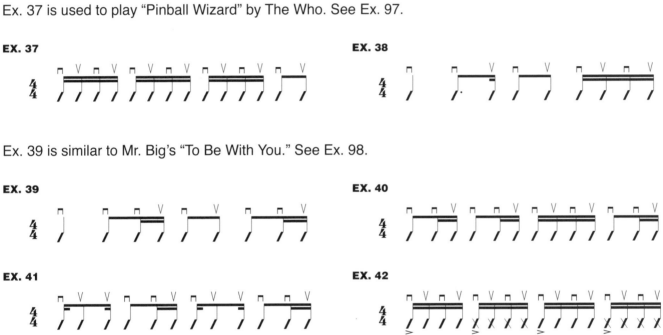

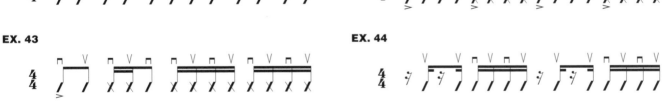

EX. 51

EX. 52

Exs. 53–64 are examples in 3/4. This means there are 3 beats (instead of 4) in a measure and the quarter note gets one beat. Ex. 53 is used to play "How Will I Ever Be Simple Again" by Richard Thompson. See Ex. 94.

EX. 53

EX. 54

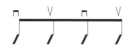

EX. 55

A variation of Ex. 56 is used by Steve Howe in Yes' "Mood For A Day." See Ex. 81.

EX. 56

Ex. 57 will get you started on The Eagles' "Hollywood Waltz." See Ex. 85.

EX. 57

A variation of Ex. 58 is used by The Eagles on "Take It To the Limit."

EX. 58

EX. 59

EX. 60

EX. 61

EX. 62

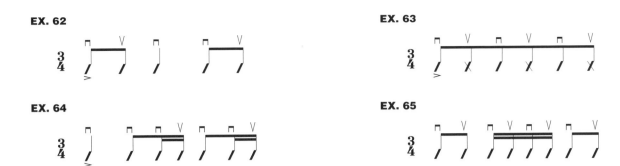

EX. 63

EX. 64

EX. 65

Exs. 66-75 explore shuffle patterns in 12/8. There are 12 beats in each measure and the eighth note gets one beat. Remember that each group of 3 beats has a triplet feel.

EX. 66

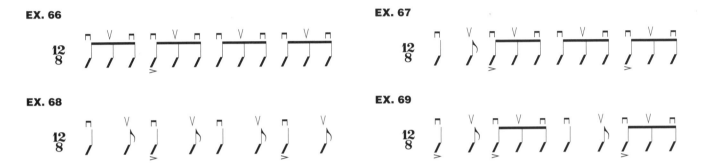

EX. 67

EX. 68

EX. 69

Ex. 70 will get you started on The Eagles' "Journey of the Sorcerer." See Ex. 90. Another variation of Ex. 70 is used by Eric Clapton on "Alberta." See Ex. 91.

EX. 70

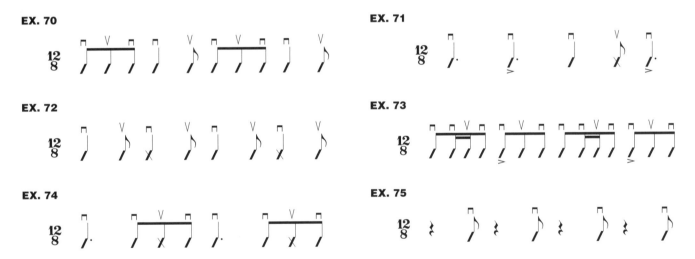

EX. 71

EX. 72

EX. 73

EX. 74

EX. 75

SONG EXAMPLES

The following are examples inspired by famous songs that feature the acoustic guitar. You'll notice that all kinds of groups and singer/songwriters have used the acoustic guitar to create legendary parts that are as indelible as any to come from a Marshall stack and a Stratocaster.

Ex. 76 is the rhythm pattern you'd use to play The Beatles' "Can't Buy Me Love."

EX. 76

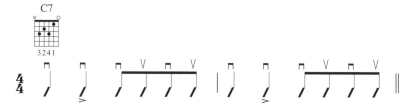

Ex. 77 is very similar to what you'd play on Rod Stewart's "Maggie May."

EX. 77

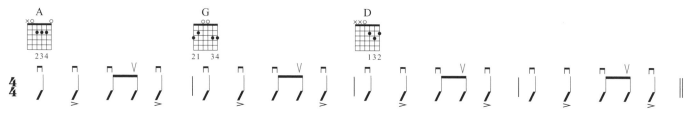

Ex. 78 sounds much like the hook in Tom Petty's "Free Fallin'."

EX. 78

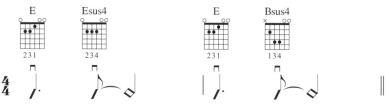

Ex. 79 will get you close to Nirvana's "Come As You Are."

EX. 79

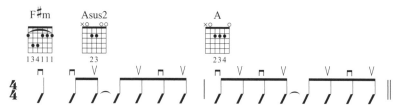

Ex. 80 echoes part of Led Zeppelin's "Babe I'm Gonna Leave You."

EX. 80

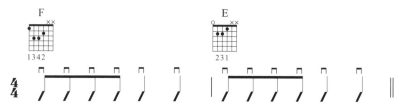

Ex. 81 reminds us of the opening to "Mood for a Day" by Yes.

EX. 81

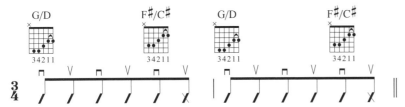

Ex. 82 is the rhythm pattern used to play "Used to Love Her" by Guns N' Roses.

EX. 82

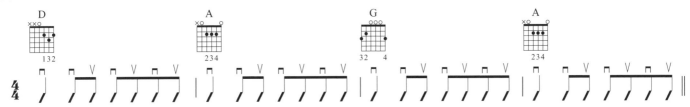

Ex. 83 is very similar to what Stephen Stills plays on "Make Love to You."

EX. 83

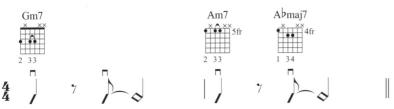

Ex. 84 sounds much like another section from "Babe I'm Gonna Leave You" by Led Zeppelin.

EX. 84

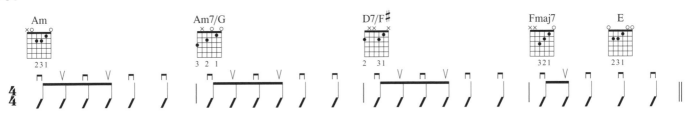

Ex. 85 may remind you of a part in "Hollywood Waltz" by The Eagles.

EX. 85

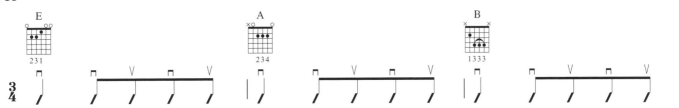

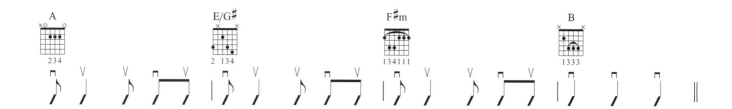

Ex. 86 was inspired by The Eagles' "Lying Eyes."

EX. 86

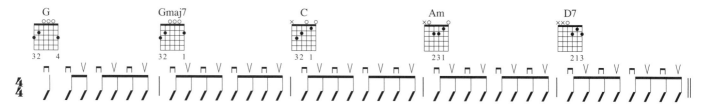

Ex. 87 echoes in the style of The Eagles' "Take It Easy."

EX. 87

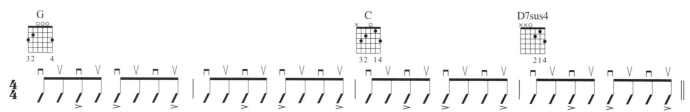

Ex. 88: The Eagles' "New Kid in Town" was the inspiration for these rhythm patterns.

EX. 88

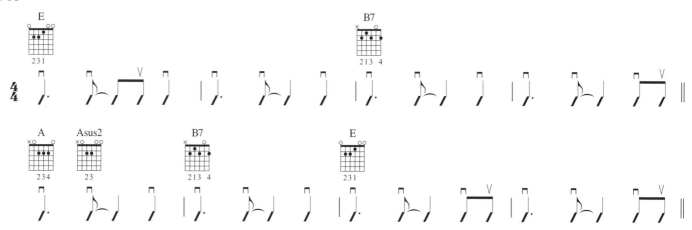

Ex. 89 reminds us of what Eric Clapton played on "San Francisco Bay Blues."

EX. 89

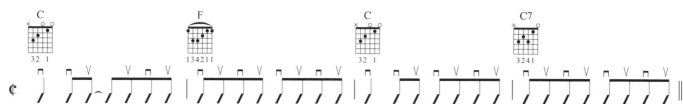

Ex. 90 was inspired by the Eagles' "Journey Of The Sorcerer."

EX. 90

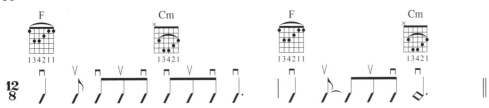

Ex. 91 has its roots in "Alberta" by Eric Clapton.

EX. 91

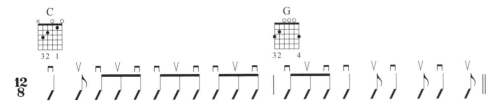

> People have told us over and over again that the acoustic songs are their favorite part of the show.
> —David Crosby (Crosby, Stills & Nash)

Exs. 92–96 use the Carter Family style, which consists of alternating bass notes with chords. It can be played using a flatpick, or by letting the thumb pick out the bass notes, while the index and middle fingers of the right-hand strum the higher strings.

Ex. 92 is reminiscent of "Rocky Raccoon" by The Beatles.

EX. 92

Ex. 93 is in the style of the opening chords from "Jessica" by The Allman Brothers Band.

EX. 93

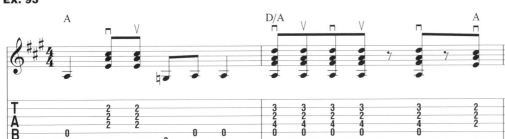

Ex. 94 is in the style of Richard Thompson's "How Will I Ever Be Simple Again."

EX. 94

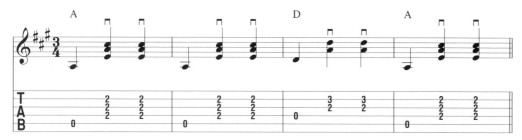

Ex. 95 has its roots in the Crosby, Stills & Nash classic, "Helplessly Hoping."

EX. 95

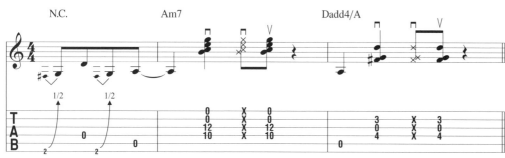

Ex. 96 is inspired by Emerson, Lake and Palmer's "From the Beginning."

EX. 96

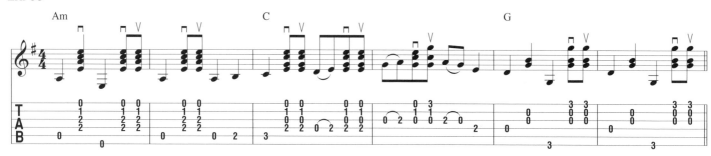

Ex. 97 became a classic move in The Who's "Pinball Wizard." To get it just right, you must play it smoothly.

EX. 97

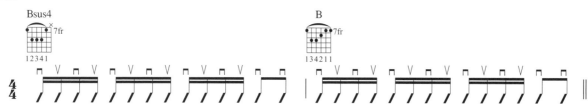

Ex. 98 was used in Mr. Big's "To Be With You."

EX. 98

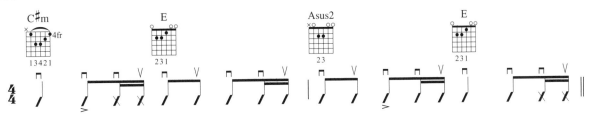

Ex. 99 was inspired by the outro to James Taylor's "Fire and Rain." Notice how changing one note from A9(no 3rd) to Asus2 can have a dramatic effect on the music.

EX. 99

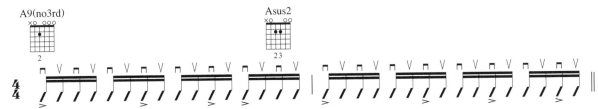

Ex. 100 is an idea we heard in Eric Clapton's "Running on Faith." Notice the progression of the second to third chords, where the inner voice is the only movement.

EX. 100

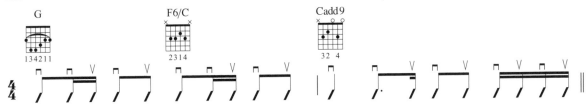

Ex. 101 has its roots in Pink Floyd's "Wish You Were Here." Notice how the first chord has the 5th in the bass note, and the second has its 3rd in the bass note, creating a smooth descending bass line.

EX. 101

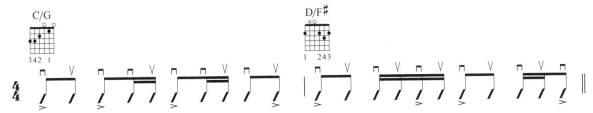

Ex. 102 was like something we heard in Sheryl Crow's "Leaving Las Vegas." The move from Dsus4 to D is one of the most popular chord changes in rock songwriting.

EX. 102

Ex. 103 was inspired by Jethro Tull's "Cheap Day Return." To play along with the record, you will need to use a capo on the 7th fret.

EX. 103

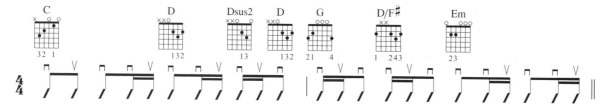

Ex. 104 comes by way of Jethro Tull's "Up to Me." It's a nice open-chord progression.

EX. 104

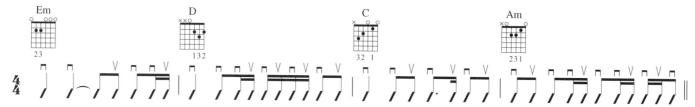

Ex. 105 has its roots in "Tangerine" by Led Zeppelin. Notice the descending bass line from one chord to another, which requires quite a stretch.

EX. 105

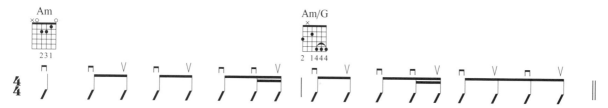

Ex. 106 was something we heard in "Gallows Pole," from Led Zeppelin, which shows movement from a major to a minor chord. This was done by changing the C♯ note to C.

EX. 106

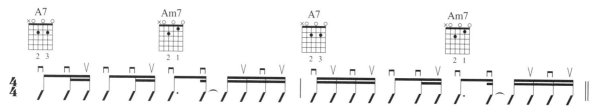

Ex. 107 is similar to a part from the Led Zeppelin classic, "Your Time is Gonna Come."

EX. 107

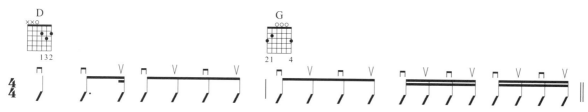

FINGERSTYLE

Fingerstyle is a popular and useful technique often used by "singer/songwriter"-type performers for playing accompaniment to their singing, or for solo guitar pieces. Most fingerstyle approaches widely used today are a product of classical and traditional folk techniques. This combination of the studied (classical) and the unschooled (folk/blues) shows you the flexibility of this style of guitar playing. That is, learn what you can, and apply it to your own music with an "anything goes" approach.

RIGHT-HAND POSITION

One way to approach the picking-hand position is to pretend that your right hand (picking hand) is lightly gripping the right handlebar of a motorcycle. Now bring your arm down so your hand is lightly touching the strings. You've got your thumb out in front of your fingers and pointed toward the neck. Your other fingers are loosely curled, and by moving your hand to a slight angle they will naturally fall into a position where the index, middle, and ring fingers each have their own string to pluck. The important thing is to play with a relaxed picking hand. So experiment until you find the position that is most comfortable for you.

Although the choice of fingering is a personal matter, we'll start with the most common fingering. The thumb will hit the bass strings (E, A, D) with a downstroke. While using upstrokes, the index finger (i) plays the G, the middle finger (m) plays the B, and the ring finger (a) plays the high E string.

Right-Hand Letters

p = thumb
i = 1st finger
m = 2nd finger
a = 3rd finger

BASIC STYLES

The following style explanations and 1-bar examples will give you an idea of how fingerpicking works. It will also help you to develop independent finger control, which is essential for this style. This foundation should make it easier to play and understand the examples we've chosen. They are all inspired from various fingerstyle songs, which in turn should be a starting point for discovering your own patterns.

Arpeggios

Arpeggios are played by holding a chord and playing one note after another in sequence, each note sounding separately.

Exs. 108 and 109 are basic arpeggio patterns. In Ex. 108, the high G and B notes are plucked simultaneously to become one sound. In Ex. 109, we suggest you play the first two notes with your thumb.

EX. 108

EX. 109

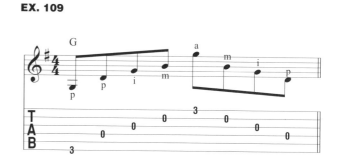

Travis Picking (Double Thumbing)

Travis picking is a technique where your thumb plays every other note. This develops a bass line on the lower strings while a melody is played on the higher strings. See Exs. 110 and 111.

EX. 110

EX. 111

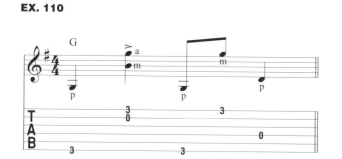

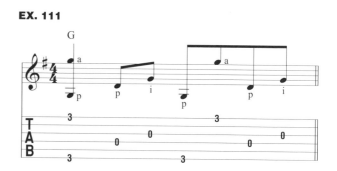

Pick and Fingers

One of the more versatile approaches to acoustic or electric playing is to use a combination of pick and fingers. Even guitarists from Eddie Van Halen to Albert Lee have put in some time with this one. Go slow and have your pick do the downstrokes while your fingers do the upstrokes. See Exs. 112 and 113.

EX. 112

EX. 113

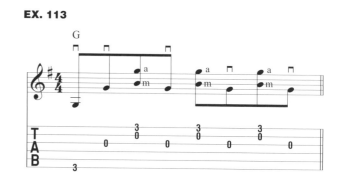

Flatpicking

In place of your fingers, you can use a pick to arpeggiate chords. Bands like Candlebox, The Black Crowes, and Gin Blossoms have used this style to good effect. Al DiMeola learned to flatpick so fast because he was trying to imitate Doc Watson, but what he didn't know was that Doc was fingerpicking his parts. At the end of the day, Al learned to duplicate Doc's fingerpicking with just a pick, and developed his own style in the process! Using that as our model, try to play all of the following examples with a pick, or any style you like. See Exs. 114 and 115.

EX. 114

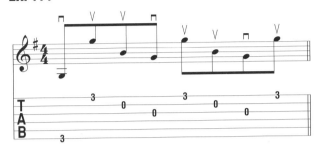

EX. 115

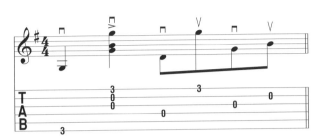

PRACTICE TIPS

1. As with strumming, it is very important to keep a smooth, steady rhythm. Playing along with a drum machine should help your timing.

2. For all of the examples, hold each chord while you are picking and let each note ring.

3. Experiment with different fingers or different picking styles. If something works better for you because it feels right, then it *is* right!

> *I don't play a lot of electric at home. I tend to play acoustic because it is my main direction.*
>
> —Steve Howe (Yes)

SONG EXAMPLES

The following are song examples that use the fingerpicking style:

Ex. 116 is the Travis-style pattern that Paul Simon used in "American Tune."

EX. 116

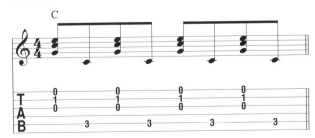

Ex. 117 is a fingerpicking pattern similar to Led Zeppelin's "Babe I'm Gonna Leave You."

EX. 117

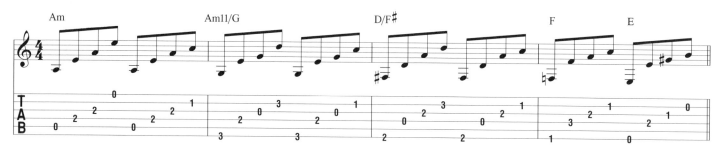

Ex. 118 is inspired by Greg Lake's fingerpicking in Emerson, Lake & Palmer's "From the Beginning."

EX. 118

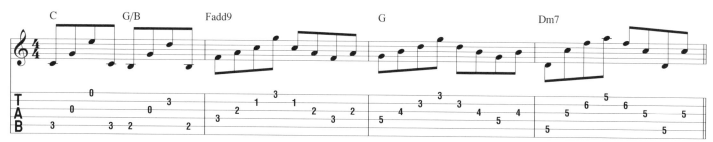

Ex. 119 has its roots in Led Zeppelin's classic, "Stairway to Heaven."

EX. 119

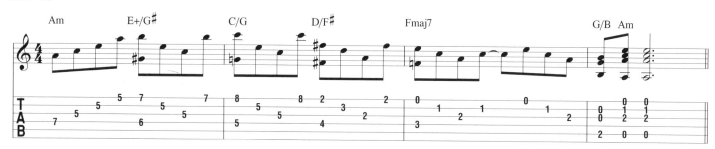

Ex. 120 is similar to Jim Croce's intro to "I'll Have to Say I Love You in a Song."

EX. 120

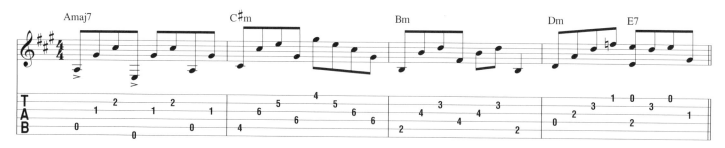

Ex. 121 was inspired by Jim Croce's "Operator."

EX. 121

Ex. 122 has its roots in the song "If" by Bread.

EX. 122

Ex. 123 is a lot like James Taylor's rendition of "You've Got a Friend."

EX. 123

Ex. 124 resembles an Al DiMeola line from "Electric Rendezvous."

EX. 124

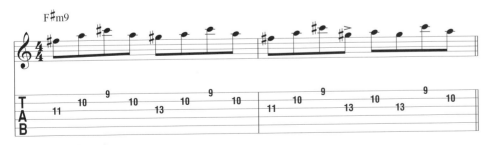

The song that gives me a kick from Appetite *is 'Brownstone.' It was written on acoustic guitar.*

—Izzy Stradlin (Guns N' Roses)

Ex. 125 was inspired by Extreme's hit, "More Than Words."

EX. 125

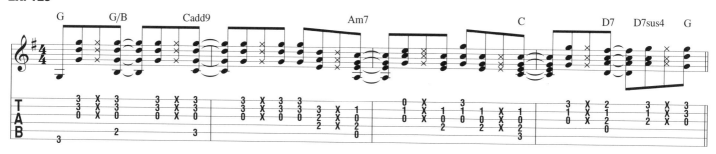

Ex. 126 echoes the opening chords of "Helplessly Hoping" from Crosby, Stills & Nash.

EX. 126

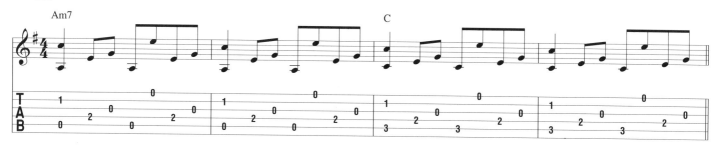

Ex. 127 was inspired by "Dust in the Wind" by Kansas. This is a good place to begin to explore your Travis picking. Over the next few examples, you'll find various illustrations of this technique.

EX. 127

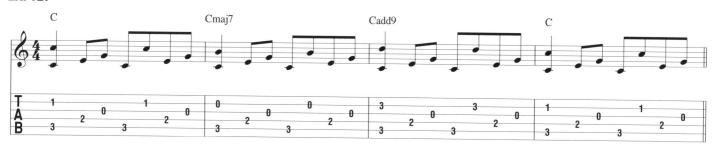

Ex. 128 is another example of Travis picking, this time reflecting the Blind Faith tune, "Can't Find My Way Home."

EX. 128

Ex. 129 is similar to the Steven Stills bit in "Haven't We Lost Enough?"

EX. 129

Ex. 130 is a take on another Stephen Stills tune, "Thoroughfare Gap."

EX. 130

Ex. 131 was inspired by Jethro Tull's "Sossity; You're a Woman."

EX. 131

Ex. 132 may remind you of Eric Clapton's "Tears in Heaven."

EX. 132

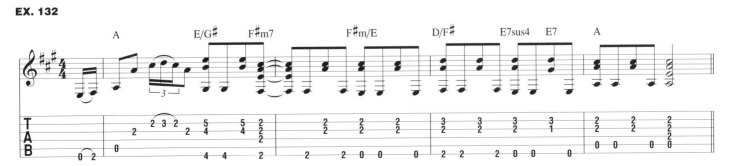

Ex. 133 resembles "Blackbird" by The Beatles.

EX. 133

Ex. 134 is similar to "Send Me An Angel" by The Scorpions.

EX. 134

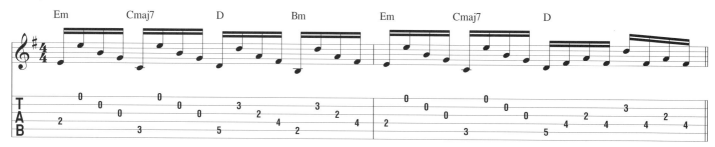

Ex. 135 was inspired by Bon Jovi's "Wanted Dead or Alive."

EX. 135

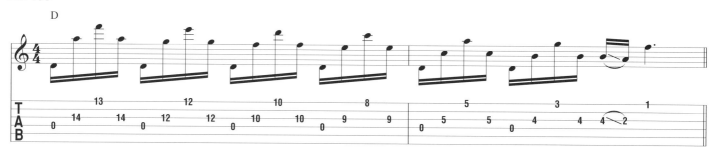

Ex. 136 is a take on Led Zeppelin's "Your Time is Gonna Come."

EX. 136

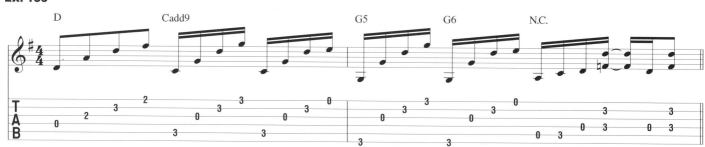

> *'Call Me the Breeze' and 'Cocaine' I wrote on an old $50 Harmony acoustic guitar.*
>
> —*J.J. Cale*

Ex. 137 is similar to Sheryl Crow's "Strong Enough."

EX. 137

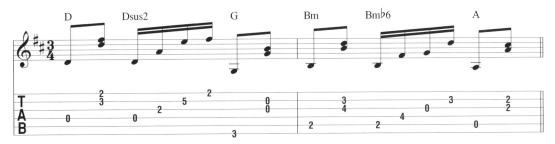

Ex. 138 resembles a line from "Passion, Grace & Fire" by John McLaughlin, Al DiMeola and Paco DeLucia.

EX. 138

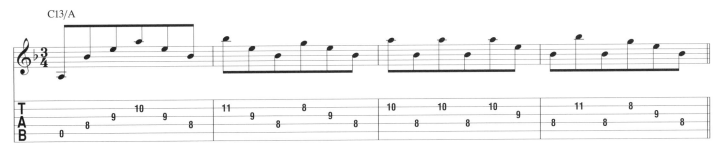

Ex. 138 was inspired by Jim Croce's "Time in a Bottle." It's a classic arpeggio figure with the bass line descending in half steps (one fret at a time).

EX. 139

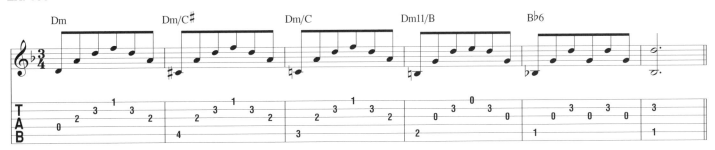

Ex. 140 is a bit of "Fluff," from Black Sabbath.

EX. 140

Since the first song I've written, it has always been done on an acoustic guitar. On the acoustic guitar, I'm more inclined to be looking for a melody within the chord structure. From a songwriter's point of view, when I sit down with an acoustic, I'm thinking melody—I'm thinking of hooks.

—Jon Bon Jovi (Bon Jovi)

Basic Blues
FOR ROCK GUITAR

INTRODUCTION

B.B. King had it right when he said, "The blues is like a mother tree. Many branches of music have sprouted from it." All forms of rock (and jazz) can trace their roots back to the blues. It's obvious in players like Eric Clapton and Stevie Ray Vaughan. But guitarists from Metallica's Kirk Hammett and Queensrÿche's Michael Wilton to Kiss' Paul Stanley have also gone to the blues for musical inspiration. And the blues, in all its many branches, has always used the guitar as its foundation. As blues guitar legend Otis Rush so aptly put it, "In blues music the guitar is kind of like a movie star. All the other instruments go with it."

Basic Blues for Rock Guitar will provide you with an easy introduction on how to play the blues progression and provide you with some classic "starter" licks to play over that progression. That's all you need to know for now. Just spend as much time as you need to with the tablature explanation and then let's play.

> *The heart of the blues never changes, but I think the sound of it does change. It's always managed to be contemporary music whatever year something comes out. It always reflects the lIfe and times of where it came from. At least 50% of the rock music you hear comes from the blues. The same with jazz, too. Blues and jazz are root American music. They will always be with us.*
>
> —John Mayall (Blues Breakers)

EXPLAINING TABLATURE

Tablature is a paint-by-number language telling you which notes to play on the fingerboard. Each of the six lines represents a string on the guitar. The numbers on the line indicate which frets to press down. Note that tablature does not indicate the rhythm.

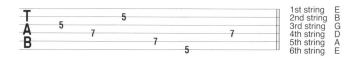

1st string	E
2nd string	B
3rd string	G
4th string	D
5th string	A
6th string	E

NOTATION LEGEND

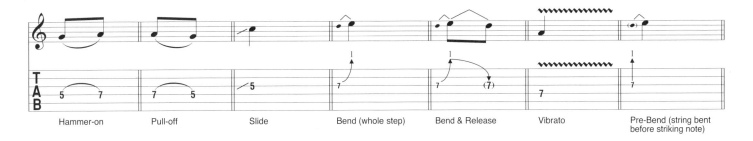

Hammer-on   Pull-off   Slide   Bend (whole step)   Bend & Release   Vibrato   Pre-Bend (string bent before striking note)

Hammer-on:

Pick the first (lower) note, then "hammer on" to sound the higher note with another finger by fretting it without picking.

Pull-off:

Place both fingers on the notes to be sounded. Pick the first (higher) note, then sound the lower note by "pulling off" the finger on the higher note while keeping the lower note fretted.

Slide:

Strike the first note, and then, without striking it again, use the same left-hand finger to slide up or down the string to the second note.

Bend (whole step):

Pick the note and bend up a whole step (two frets).

Bend & Release:

Pick the note and bend up a whole step, then release the bend back to the original note. All three notes are tied together; only the first note is attacked.

Vibrato:

Vibrate the note by rapidly bending and releasing the string using a left-hand finger, wrist, or forearm.

Finger Number:

Suggested fingerings are included under the tab staff for all examples. However, you should experiment with different fingerings and play the one that feels most comfortable to you.

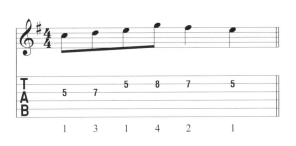

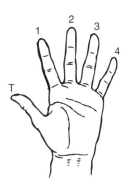

T = thumb
1 = 1st finger
2 = 2nd finger
3 = 3rd finger
4 = 4th finger

All of the examples in this book are written in one key (A), and are commonly played over an A blues. Practice each lick very slowly, until you can play them very smoothly. Play a cool lick sloppily and people will hear the slop, not the lick.

THE 12-BAR BLUES

Ex. 1 is the basic 12-bar blues progression in A. Presented in its simplest form, this song structure is commonly called the I (one), IV (four), V (five) blues progression. This simple, repeated, three-chord progression is the foundation for blues songwriting, and many forms of rock music as well. The A, or I chord, plays straight through the first four bars. This is followed by two bars of D, the IV chord. We go back to A (I) for two more bars and follow it with two bars of E, the V chord. We end back at the A or I chord. This progression can be heard in tunes like "Scuttle Buttin" and "Love Struck Baby" (Stevie Ray Vaughan), "Keep Your Hands to Yourself" (Georgia Satellites), and, in a repeated riff form, in The Beatles tune "Birthday." This is also the pattern used on the mother of all rock 'n' roll songs, "Johnny B. Goode" (Chuck Berry, Jimi Hendrix, Johnny Winter, The Grateful Dead, Judas Priest, etc.)

EX. 1

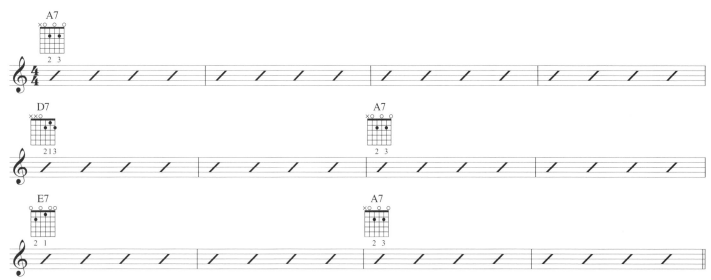

> *When we first came together; we had a gig in a week. We had never played together so we learned eighteen 12-bar blues numbers in a week. It was great practice for learning how to play. It was a great way of going into what we play now. You keep playing all the 12 bars and you could start experimenting around those three chords.*
> *—Tony Iommi (Black Sabbath)*

Ex. 2 is the most common of the many variations of Ex. 1. The difference between these two examples is the use of the IV (D) chord in the 2nd and 10th measures, and the addition of the V (E) in the 12th measure. It is used as you see it here in songs like "Sweet Little Angel" (B.B. King), "Ice Cream Man" (Van Halen), "Statesboro Blues" (The Allman Brothers, Taj Mahal) "The Sky Is Crying" (Stevie Ray Vaughan), 'Tush' (ZZ Top), and "Before You Accuse Me" (Eric Clapton), among countless others. Songs like "T-Bone Shuffle" (Albert Collins, Robert Cray, and Johnny Copeland) and "Slow Down" (Carl Perkins, The Beatles) use this same progression with the exception of the last measure, which stays on the I (A).

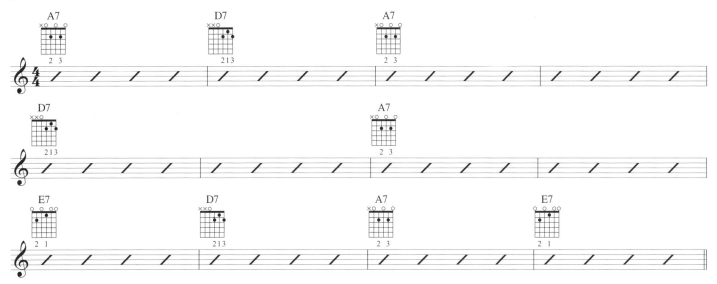

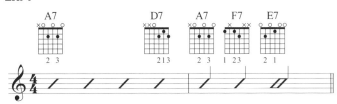

> *Knowing that you only have three chord changes in most of the 12- bar blues you've got to be kind of like a woman who knows many tricks about making love. You can't stay on the one chord and let it be dead. You've got to find something to color each passage that leads to the next chord. Think about it, you've got four bars before you make a change.*
>
> *— B.B. King*

Exs. 3-7 present several variations on the *turnaround*, the last two bars of the progression.

EX. 3

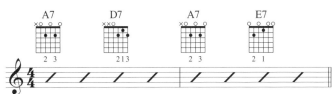

EX. 4

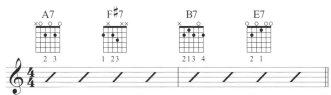

EX. 5

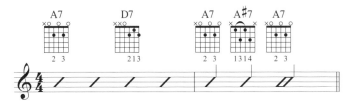

EX. 6

EX. 7

Now that you know the mechanics of the basic blues progression, let's put some feel into it. How you play these chords will set the mood and the groove of the song. Your rhythm attack is what makes the song rock or swing. You can downstrum four times (one per beat) in each bar, as presented in Ex. 8. Or you can just play beats one and three, as shown in Ex. 9. This one was inspired by The Allman Brothers rhythm part in "Done Somebody Wrong." The sound is short and crisp, exactly like clapping your hands on beats one and three. Instead of clapping, just play the chords.

EX. 8

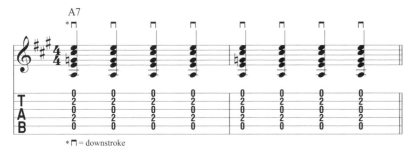

* ⊓ = downstroke

EX. 9

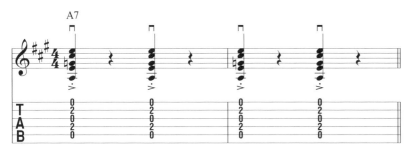

Ex. 10 is the 12-bar blues progression played in a shuffle rhythm. This is the rhythm used in "Johnny B. Goode." If you simplify this part down to one chord and play straight eighth notes, it sounds like the jackhammer rhythms of Metallica as presented in Ex. 11. Play this Metallica-like example with a shuffle feel and you've found the roots of rock 'n' roll. See Ex. 12.

EX. 10

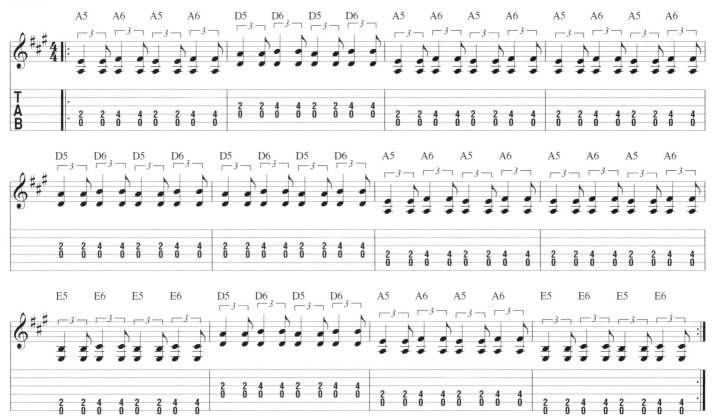

EX. 11

EX. 12

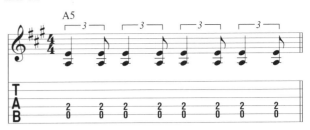

Ex. 13 is a variation of Ex. 10, used in such songs as "Roll Over Beethoven," "Sweet Little Sixteen," and "Kansas City." This is the stuff that The Beatles got started with.

EX. 13

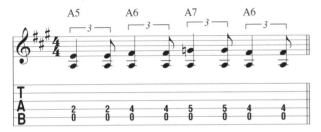

> *Back during the Jokers, in the early '60s, I was doing copy stuff and playing a lot of blues. I was singing "Stormy Monday" and did a lot of Lonnie Mack tunes. I was going through a real learning process.*
>
> —Dickie Betts (The Allman Brothers Band)

BLUES RIFFS

This first group of blues licks are short one-bar phrases. With few exceptions, they will work against any chord in the progression. This means you can play them anywhere you want in the A blues progressions we've already outlined. These types of licks are often used to punctuate a song. You can use call and response to answer a vocal line. The vocalist sings their line (call) and the guitarist answers them (response) right away. These licks can also be used as part of an extended solo.

Ex. 14 is a classic blues move that is often used by Eric Clapton. No doubt he copped it from the blues masters that inspired him. The second, third, and fourth notes spell out an A chord, which clearly define both the chord and the key we are playing in. You may find it helpful to barre your first finger on the B and E strings when playing the third and fourth notes of this line.

EX. 14

Ex.15 is one of our favorite B.B King-influenced licks, so often used in playing blues lines.

EX. 15

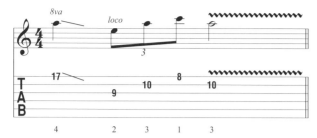

Ex. 16 is another simple B.B. King-inspired line. After you have this lick down, try mixing up the order of the notes. Any way you play them, these notes will sound good together.

EX. 16

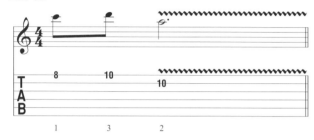

Ex. 17 is yet another simple B.B. King-like line. This one uses the pull-off. The first three notes of this lick stand up as a classic on their own. You've heard one variation of this in Jimmy Page's "Stairway to Heaven" solo.

EX. 17

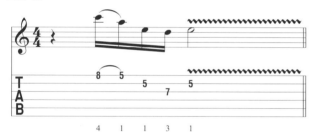

Ex. 18 is similar to an Eric Clapton lick from the *Layla* version of "Have You Ever Loved A Woman." Originally played in the same key we are using here, this lick incorporates bend and release, and vibrato techniques. It works nicely when changing from the IV chord to the I chord.

EX. 18

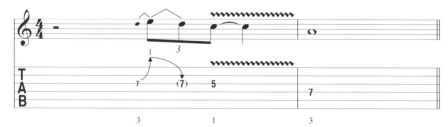

> *Albert and B.B. King have always been my biggest influences. I've never been interested in the technical side of ability. I love guitar players that can't even play just for their feel.*
> —Robin Trower

Ex. 19 has its roots in the same song as Ex. 18 and is also a nice lick to follow it, because it works well on the I chord.

EX. 19

Ex. 20 was influenced from a line in the Led Zeppelin blues classic, "Since I've Been Lovin' You."

EX. 20

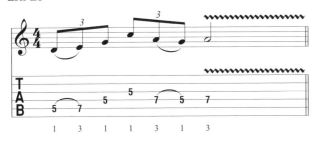

Ex.21 is a blues cliché as interpreted by guitar greats from Clapton and Vaughan to all three Kings (B.B., Albert and Freddie, who are not related).

EX. 21

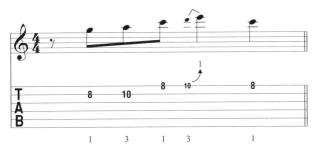

Ex. 22 is a lick similar to something we heard in Clapton's hit song "Forever Man." Using this pattern, move up three frets, to the 8th fret, and you will be in the same key (C) as the original lick, If you play these same four notes in a different order, with a different rhythm, you can figure out the opening riff to "Layla."

EX. 22

> *You don't have to grow up to understand the blues. You can always get it. I always remember getting it, but I didn't want to implement it. I always wanted to play faster because it was more impressive. Eddie Van Halen is basically a blues guitar player with modern-day flash and a wang bar.*
> *—Vivian Campbell (Dio, Whitesnake, Def Leppard)*

Ex. 23 has its roots in a Van Halen lick.

EX. 23

Ex. 24 was inspired by a line Dickie Betts played in The Allman Brothers' rendition of "Stormy Monday."

EX. 24

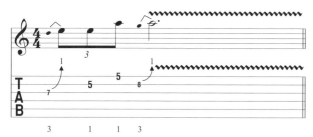

Ex. 25 is yet another of the great blues lines that has been "adopted" by players from Johnny Winter to Buddy Guy.

EX. 25

Ex. 26 was inspired by David Gilmour's playing on the Pink Floyd classic "Another Brick In The Wall, Part 2." Gilmour is a master of playing straight blues licks in settings outside the familiar blues progression. Using this pattern, move up five frets, to the 10th fret, and you will be in the same key (D) as the original lick.

EX. 26

Ex. 27 is a blues cliché adopted by generations of players from Johnny Winter to Mike McCready.

EX. 27

Ex. 28 is a string bending lick from Eric Clapton's "Forever Man."

EX. 28

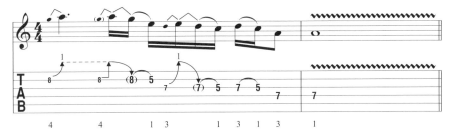

Ex. 29 features the use of barred notes to begin the riff and follows it with bending and releasing, and a pull-off.

EX. 29

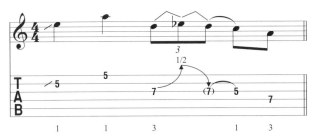

Ex. 30 is a descending Clapton-like line that works particularly well on the I chord.

EX. 30

This Clapton-influenced lick focuses on bending and vibrato.

EX. 31

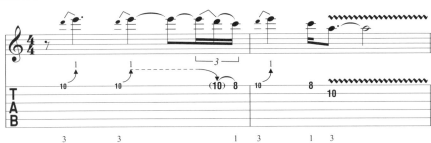

Ex. 32 is a unison bend take on a Johnny Winter line from "Be Careful with a Fool." This unison bend is one of the standard techniques for rock and blues guitar players. Using this pattern, move up three frets to the 8th fret, and you will be in the same key (C) as the original lick.

EX. 32

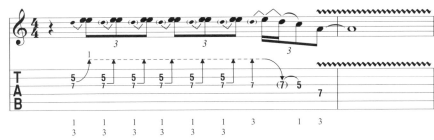

Ex. 33 is another unison bend riff, this time inspired by Eric Clapton.

EX. 33

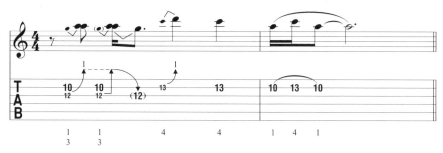

Ex. 34 is a standard blues riff. You'll notice that most of these riffs end on the root note A. This is a common practice for playing the blues in any key. Most of the time you will end your riff on the root (key) note.

EX. 34

Ex. 35 is a T-Bone Walker-like line that is just right for moving from the V chord to the I chord.

EX. 35

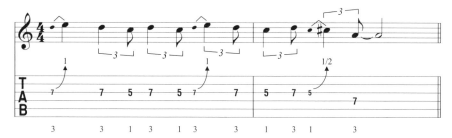

Ex. 36 is a Clapton-like line that is best used moving from the IV chord to the I chord.

EX. 36

> *Howlin' Wolf wrote some pretty heavy riffs. Back then, "Smokestack Lightning"*
> *was considered punky and dirty and lowdown. It was the Devil's music. Those*
> *blues people were getting the same bad rap a lot of people try to hang on us*
> *right now. If you turned it up and played it aggressively, 'Smokestack Lightning"*
> *is basically a heavy metal song.*
>
> *—Kirk Hammett (Metallica)*

Ex. 37 is a T-Bone Walker-inspired take on the same idea of moving from the IV chord to the I chord. Playing this lick, you can see how T-Bone was a major link between jazz and blues.

EX. 37

Ex. 38 has its roots in Clapton's fiery playing on "All Your Love," from the legendary Blues Breakers album. Check out his use of the E♭, the "blue note" of the A Blues Scale.

EX. 38

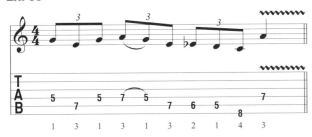

Ex. 39 was inspired by an Otis Rush line from "All Your Love."

EX. 39

Ex. 40 is a classic touch of blues inspired by the guitar style of Stevie Ray Vaughan.

EX. 40

Ex.41 is a chromatic lick inspired by B.B. King. Chromatic means playing in half steps (one fret apart), as played from the 1st through 5th notes of this lick.

EX. 41

Ex. 42 is another chromatic lick (notes 7-10), this one inspired by Dickie Betts on "Stormy Monday."

EX. 42

Ex. 43 is a descending, B.B. King-like line designed for a chord change from the I (A) to the IV (D).

EX. 43

This double-stop slide, commonly used by The Allman Brothers and Johnny Winter is perfect for moving from the I chord to the IV chord.

EX. 44

Ex. 45 is a Clapton-like line that was designed for the IV chord. The D7 chord will sound more effective if you play it staccato (short with accent).

EX. 45

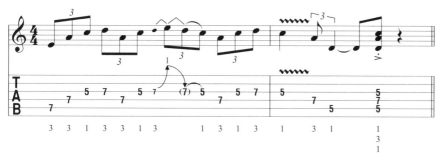

Ex. 46 is a Stevie Ray Vaughan-like lick that also works for the IV chord.

EX. 46

Ex. 47 and Ex. 48 are Stevie Ray Vaughan-inspired lines using the lower strings.

EX. 47

EX. 48

Ex. 49 is an Eric Clapton-inspired line that works well going from the IV chord to the I chord.

EX. 49

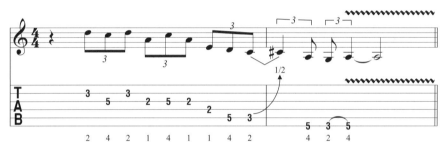

Ex. 50 is similar to a Jimi Hendrix riff from "Red House." Bending notes is one of the most important stylistic devices in blues guitar playing. You may want to go back over the riffs you already know, and anytime a note is followed by another note two frets away (a whole step), try bending to the second note instead of hammering-on, picking, or sliding to it.

EX. 50

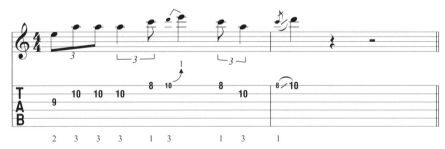

Ex. 51 is in the style of Eric Clapton.

EX. 51

Ex. 52 is a set of repeating triplets (three notes to a beat) similar to a riff by Jimi Hendrix in his rendition of Earl King's "Come On." This starts our section on longer blues riffs.

EX. 52

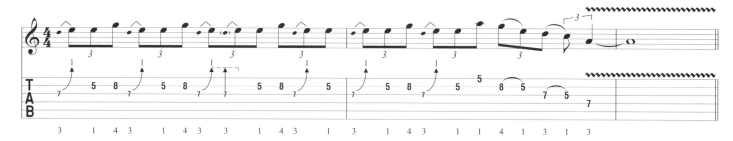

Ex. 53 is reminiscent of a line played in the Pearl Jam song "Once."

EX. 53

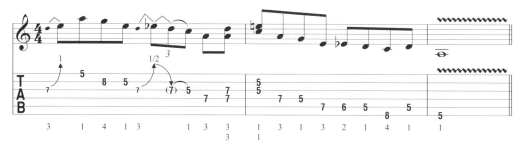

Ex. 54 was inspired by a Stevie Ray Vaughan riff featuring bends, hammer-ons, and pull-offs.

EX. 54

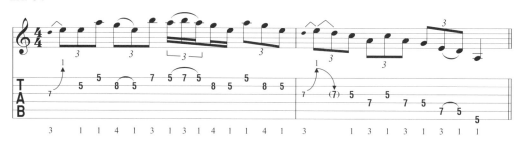

Ex. 55 is essentially a descending line much like what David Gilmour played in "Another Brick In The Wall, Part 2."

EX. 55

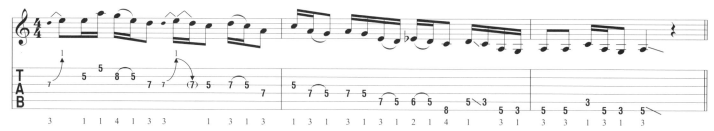

> *B.B. King and Mike Bloomfield in particular really turned me onto guitar. Jimi Hendrix took it one step further, but I recognized immediately that Jimi was a blues guitar player.*
> —Pat Simmons (The Doobie Brothers)

> *Anybody can play a blues lick, but it's not going to be done right unless it's done for real. Billy Gibbons and Albert Collins play with so much conviction behind every lick that you can't help but believe them.*
> —Greg Howe

TURNAROUNDS

The next set of examples are played exclusively over the last two bars of the 12-bar blues progression. These last two bars are called the *turnaround*. It acts as a closing statement and turns the music around to get you ready for the next repetition of the progression. There are innumerable ways to play a turnaround. The fact is, every time you get to the last two bars in the progression, you have a new opportunity to reinvent the turnaround. Here are ten of them to get you started.

Ex. 56 is in the style of an Allman Brothers turnaround from "Stormy Monday."

EX. 56

Ex. 57 is a classic string skipping turnaround you'll probably recognize from countless blues tunes.

EX. 57

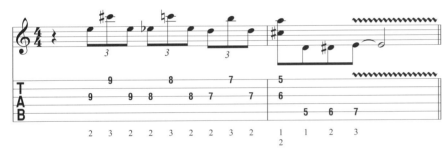

Ex. 58 is another well-known turnaround.

EX. 58

Ex. 59 is like a turnaround Alvin Lee might have done in Ten Years After's "I'm Goin' Home." It's a perfect fit to be played over Ex. 3.

EX. 59

Ex. 60 is a Clapton-like turnaround for the chord changes: A7—D7 I A7—E7 I.

EX. 60

Ex. 61 is in the style of John Hall, taken from the Orleans song "Sweet Johanna."

EX. 61

Ex. 62 is a Johnny Winter-inspired turnaround.

EX. 62

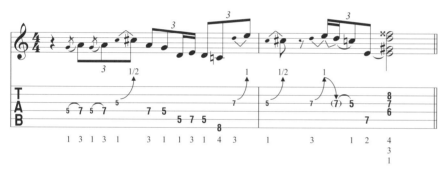

Ex. 63 picks up on ideas Gary Moore played in a turnaround from "Since I Met You Baby."

EX. 63

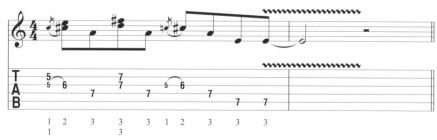

> I went back to my blues roots. I searched for what got me started playing guitar in the first place. Those old blues players (like Elmore James) were really just heart and soul. Jamming with the blues is just pure expression.
> —Michael Wilton (Queensrÿche)

Ex. 64 is considered a classic. It was inspired by an Eric Clapton turnaround in "Key to the Highway."

EX. 64

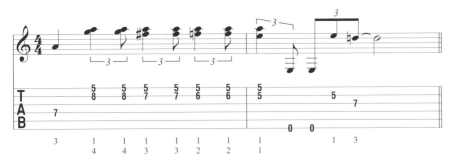

Ex. 65 is a variation of Ex. 42 and another take on a familiar Eric Clapton turnaround.

EX. 65

> I love to play the blues. I'll jam with friends out in the garage. Of course I don't have any friends. Nowadays I play with my drum machine. My favorite blues guitarists are the usual guys, B.B. King, Hubert Sumlin, Eric Clapton, Otis Rush, and of course, Jimi Hendrix.
>
> —Walter Becker (Steely Dan)

Ex. 66 is a solo that contains some of the licks presented in this book. Above the musical notation, you will see Roman numerals, which tell you what positions to play in. After the high opening A, the solo kicks in at the 8th position. As you play through the solo, be aware of how all of these short phrases come together to make a longer, more coherent statement.

Playing a guitar solo is the most personal form of expression on the instrument. While we share the same basic scales and patterns with greats like Eric Clapton, Jimi Hendrix, and Albert King, it is the way we make the notes speak that defines the individual artist. Anyone can be a stylist, you just have to discover your own voice on the instrument. Remember that the TAB, fingerings, and phrasing (hammer-on, slides, vibrato, etc.) are merely suggestions; a place to start. Take these ideas and play them with your own voice.

Solo Notes:

- The opening pickup lick and meas. 1 is Ex. 15.
- Meas. 3 is a variation of Ex. 23.
- Meas. 4, 5 and 6 use licks inspired by Gary Moore's live solo in "Since I Met You Baby."
- Meas. 9, 10 and 11 is a variation of Ex. 63. It's the same riff played in the 12th, 10th, and 5th positions.
- Meas. 12 is a turnaround coming from Ex. 56.
- Feel free to play any turnaround you like.

ABOUT THE A BLUES SCALES

The Blues Scale and the Minor Pentatonic Scale are the most common sources for rock and blues guitar solos. Artists from Muddy Waters to Metallica dip into the same pool of notes you have explored in the previous examples. The A Blues Scale is essentially the same as the A Minor Pentatonic Scale with the addition of one note. The A Minor Pentatonic Scale consists of five notes from the A Natural Minor Scale (A,B,C,D,E,F,G). These notes are: A (Root), C (♭3rd), D (4th), E (5th), and G (♭7th).

To turn the A Minor Pentatonic Scale into the A Blues Scale you add one note, the ♭5 (E♭). So the A Blues Scale is comprised of A, C, D, E♭(D♯), E and G. This additional note gives the scale a distinctively bluesy sound. That's why it's called a "blue note."

The A Blues Scale is presented here in five basic patterns found throughout the neck. There are also suggested fingerings to get you started. Once you feel comfortable with the individual patterns, try connecting them. Play them on one or perhaps two strings. The more ways you have of connecting the patterns, the more you will be comfortable creating your own blues licks throughout the entire length of the neck. Pattern 2 is the most common pattern for the A Blues Scale, and, as you might have already noticed, the most prominent pattern used in our examples. To learn more about how blues licks fit into all these patterns, you should look into the following chapters on Major and Minor Pentatonic Scales for Guitar.

5 BASIC PATTERNS OF THE A BLUES SCALE

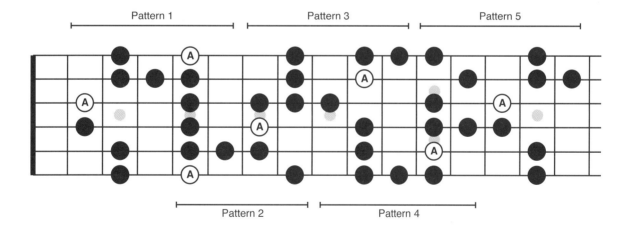

Pattern 1

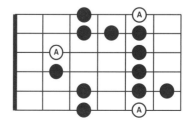

Pattern 2

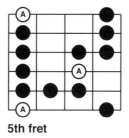

5th fret

Pattern 3

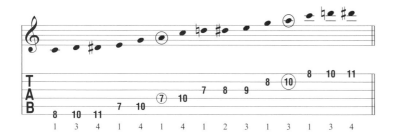
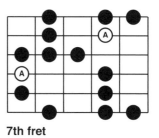

7th fret

Pattern 4

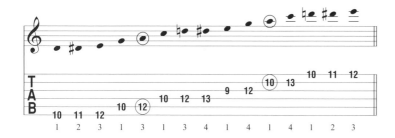
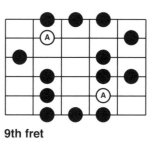

9th fret

Pattern 5

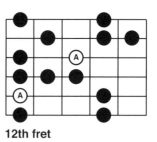

12th fret

> *If you can feel the hurt, you can play the blues. My roots are definitely black blues. I spent 13 years of my life in Journey trying to play guitar, and just by playing a blues solo with Michael Bolton on "Dock of the Bay," everybody goes wow!*
>
> —Neal Schon (Journey)

TRANSPOSING

Ex. 67 is a repeat of Ex. 25 in A blues. But what if you want to play the same lick or pattern in D blues? Since D is located five frets up from A, we simply move the same lick or pattern up five frets, in this case to the 10th fret.

EX. 67

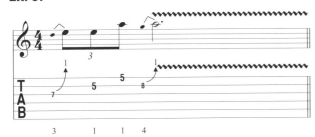

Ex. 68 is the exact same lick as Ex. 25, only now you're playing the lick transposed to the D Blues Scale. This is one common way to transpose. Pick a lick from anywhere in the book and move it up five frets. Play it exactly the same, and you're playing in D blues. Pick another A blues lick from anywhere on the neck, but this time move up three frets. Now you are playing in C blues. Why? Because the new root note, C is located three frets away from A. Pick any lick in A blues, move it down two frets, and you're playing it in G blues.

EX. 68

So if you want to transpose (move) a lick from the A Blues Scale to another key, locate your new root note on either E string, or any string you choose. Count how many frets up or down it is from the original root note A, and move the riff up or down the same number of frets. Refer to the diagram from the previous section (the patterns presented on the neck) to learn where the roots of each scale pattern can be found on all the strings. You may use a root note on any string to transpose.

The following diagram shows you how this rule works. You can see what it looks like when you transpose from the 5th-position A Blues Scale to the 10th position D Blues Scale.

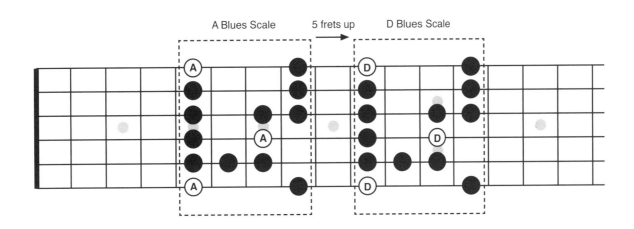

RECOMMENDED LISTENING

The following is a list for some recommended blues/rock listening. We feel this partial list of recordings have been both essential and influential in helping to shape generations of rock guitar players. These particular recordings were chosen for their classic blues content.

A Man and the Blues — Buddy Guy
Appetite for Destruction — Slash
Back in Black— Angus Young
Bridge of Sighs — Robin Trower
Cat Scratch Fever — Ted Nugent
Crusade with John Mayall's Blues Breakers — Mick Taylor
Dire Straits — Mark Knopfler
Electric Rag (Best of) — Mike Bloomfield
Electric Ladyland — Jimi Hendrix
Exile On Mainstreet — Keith Richards
Free (Best of) — Paul Kossoff
Hard Road with John Mayall's Blues Breakers — Peter Green
In Step — Stevie Ray Vaughan
John Mayall's Blues Breakers with Eric Clapton — Eric Clapton
Led Zeppelin II — Jimmy Page
Live at the Fillmore East — The Allman Brothers Band
Live at the Regal— B.B. King
Live Wire/Blues Power — Albert King
Moonflower — Santana
Muddy Waters on Chess (Best of)— Muddy Waters
One Foot in the Blues — ZZ Top
Over the Top (Mountain) — Leslie West
Plaid — Blues Saraceno
Second Winter — Johnny Winter
See the Light — Jeff Healey
Still Got the Blues — Gary Moore
Strange Pleasure — Jimmy Vaughan
Surfing wIth the Allen — Joe Satriani
Takin' My Time — Bonnie Raitt
Talk To Your Daughter — Robben Ford
Toys in the Attic — Joe Perry
Truth — Jeff Beck
Waiting For Columbus — Lowell George

Some final thoughts on the blues...

I never lose track of the fact that I am a blues player. It is the most expressive form I know on the guitar.
—Jeff Beck

The kind of guitar playing that I was into was the blues style and this feeling. That's not something you can practice and learn. It's something you get from listening to records and jamming with other people. You can't sit down and just practice burning through blues scales. It's not going to do you any good. You really have to do it. You have to play with other people, listen to it, be exposed to it. It's not as much a technical thing as it is a feeling thing.

—Tom Keifer (Cinderella)

The 12-bar blues is a deceivingly difficult form of music. At one point, when I first heard blues, I thought, "How many times can you play the same damn thing?" Well, there is an infinite amount of ways to play it. It all comes down to interpretation, tone, and dynamics. Phrasing is the key, in the same way phrasing is the key to a singer; how much you put into a note, how much you lay back. It comes down to making a guitar talk and sing. When it works it's pretty amazing. I remember seeing Buddy Guy in the late '60s and it thrilled me. I had seen Hendrix and he made me want to go further back to Howlin' Wolf and Muddy Waters. And although I appreciate them, it wasn't until people started really singing on the electric guitar that the blues really got me.

—Paul Stanley (Kiss)

Let me borrow a quote from Keith Richards. He said, "It may be the same three chords, but let's just figure out a new way to present it." Just about the time you think that it's all been done, then you say "What about this way?" So there is perhaps the possibility of endless variations on a theme that doesn't necessarily need improvement. We can be bold enough to say there is a certain fairness when you allow blues to be a changing art form. Yeah, there's a blues museum, but they leave the back door open so the fresh air can continue to breeze through. Let's lean on blues as that comfortable cornerstone, which we can spring forward from, and anything goes.

—Billy Gibbons (ZZ Top)

The blues I was playing was pentatonic, but it wasn't the blues feel. There's nothing wrong with that, but I wanted to be more authentic. Old bluesmen would come up to me and say, 'I bet you can't play the blues.' I'd play my version of the blues and they'd say, 'Nope, I didn't think so.' So I decided to find out what they were talking about. But I don't think you have to be sad to play the blues. I was 11 or 12 when I saw The Band's *The Last Waltz*. That's when I got into Clapton. I said, 'Wow, what's going on?'"

—Jason Becker

I learned solos backwards and forwards. One thing I had myself learn, when I was 14, is the solo off of "Have You Heard," from The Blues Breakers album with Eric Clapton. It's a very emotional solo. The genius of Eric Clapton is that he has managed to take all of the major blues elements and fuse them together. I'm not saying he was a copy artist—I think he is a genius. Learning solos like that is so beneficial to the beginning guitar player. I know a lot of guys who say, 'I don't want to copy anybody's solo.' You can hear it. They suffer because they start off with no background. They try and let their fingers and an undeveloped musical background do the work for them. They can't. The music needs the background.

—Jeff Healey

In the early days, when I started going to see the blues players, it was probably Johnny Winter, because he was still doing it in kind of a rock format.

—Joe Perry (Aerosmith)

Jimmy Page was turned onto the guitar by blues guys. They didn't care if it was in tune or not, they just did it. There was a real atmosphere about that.

—Rik Emmett (Triumph)

Feel-wise, the first ZZ Top record would probably give you a whole perspective on blues-based rock.

—George Lynch (Dokken)

The blues is basic. The people use all these basics to do whatever they do. Like when they made the first automobile, it was probably like the wagon. It didn't have no motor, the horse was the motor. Then they made the motor, and the next guy put the windshield wipers on. The next added lights. They kept adding to it. The blues is the basic, and everything in American music has been built onto this basic of the blues.

—Willie Dixon

Major Pentatonic Scales
FOR GUITAR

INTRODUCTION

Pentatonic scales are the single most important building blocks for the rock guitar soloist. They are at the heart of all rock scales and the foundation upon which greats from Eric Clapton and Jimi Hendrix to Eddie Van Halen, Diamond Darrell and Eric Johnson have built their styles.

The word *Pentatonic* has Greek origins. *Penta* means five and *Tonic* means tone. So we've got five notes (or tones) that make up the Pentatonic scale. That's all you need to know for now. Just spend as much time as you need with the tablature explanation and let's play.

EXPLAINING TABLATURE

Tablature is a paint-by-number language telling you which notes to play on the fingerboard. Each of the six lines represents a string on the guitar. The numbers on the line indicate which frets to press down. Note that tablature does not indicate the rhythm.

1st string	E
2nd string	B
3rd string	G
4th string	D
5th string	A
6th string	E

NOTATION LEGEND

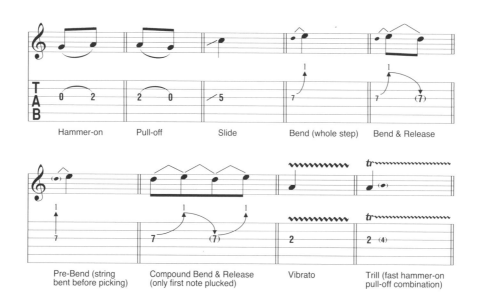

Hammer-on Pull-off Slide Bend (whole step) Bend & Release

Pre-Bend (string bent before picking) Compound Bend & Release (only first note plucked) Vibrato Trill (fast hammer-on pull-off combination)

Hammer-on:

Pick the first (lower) note, then "hammer on" to sound the higher note with another finger by fretting it without picking.

Pull-off:

Place both fingers on the notes to be sounded. Pick the first (higher) note, then sound the lower note by "pulling off" the finger on the higher note while keeping the lower note fretted.

Slide:

Strike the first note, and then, without striking it again, use the same left-hand finger to slide up or down the string to the second note.

Bend (whole step):

Pick the note and bend up a whole step (two frets).

Bend & Release:

Pick the note and bend up a whole step, then release the bend back to the original note. All three notes are tied together; only the first note is attacked.

Vibrato:

Vibrate the note by rapidly bending and releasing the string using a left-hand finger, wrist, or forearm.

Finger Number:

Suggested fingerings are included under the tab staff for all examples. However, you should experiment with different fingerings and play the one that feels most comfortable to you.

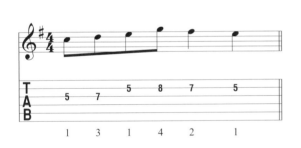

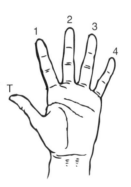

T = thumb
1 = 1st finger
2 = 2nd finger
3 = 3rd finger
4 = 4th finger

All examples in this book are presented in the A Major Pentatonic Scale. Practice each lick very slowly, until you can play them very smoothly. Play a cool lick sloppily and people will hear the slop, not the lick.

Before you dive into the A Major Pentatonic Scale, we offer this sound advice from some guitarists who got there first:

My theory is to practice two hours everyday You don't see the improvement immediately, but when you compare yourself to where you were a year before, you can be surprised. You can see that you are still progressing.
—Michael Schenker (Scorpions, UFO, MSG)

I've met a lot of players that have great ability, but they are kind of sterile. I'm a blues-based rock guitar player; and I play from emotion.
—Ace Frehley (Kiss)

Jamming with someone helps your playing a lot more than just playing by yourself in a room.
—Kirk Hammett (Metallica)

PATTERN 1

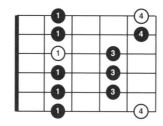

Ex. 1 was inspired by Mick Ronson's solo in David Bowie's hit song, "Suffragette City." The original solo was also played in the same key we are using here.

EX. 1

Ex. 2 is a variation of a timeless lick The Allman Brothers played on Blind Willie McTell's classic, "Statesboro Blues." Using this pattern, move up ten frets to the 12th fret, and you will then be in the same key as the original recording. In the section on transposing at the end of this chapter is a simple explanation of how you can take our examples presented in A Major Pentatonic and easily transpose them to different keys; in this case, G Major Pentatonic. As with all of the examples shown in this book, a portion of each line may appeal to you. Feel free to take each example apart and reassemble it in any way that sounds good to your ear.

EX. 2

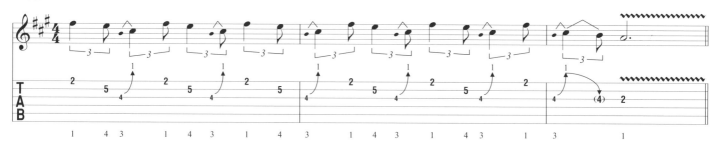

Ex.'s 3 and 4 are inspired by Carlos Santana and Neal Schon's melodic duet from "Song of the Wind." Using this pattern, move up three frets to the 5th fret, and you will be in the same key (C Major Pentatonic) as the original lick.

EX. 3

EX. 4

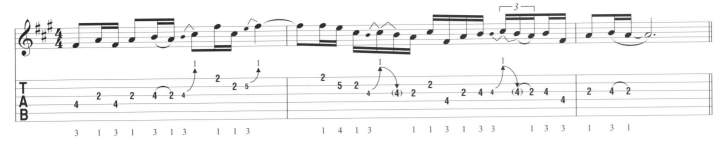

Ex. 5 is a descending lick, reminiscent of a Michael Schenker line from his instrumental "Captain Nemo." Notice the fingering in the third measure. The 3rd finger is rolled to play two consecutive notes on the same fret, different strings. If this doesn't work for you, try using your 3rd and 2nd fingers instead. Using this pattern, move up nine frets to the 11th fret, and you will be in the same key (F♯ Major Pentatonic) as the original lick. And take a tip from Michael, make playing smoothly part of your style.

EX. 5

Ex. 6 is a lick à la Nuno Bettencourt from Extreme's "Mutha (Don't Wanna Go to School Today.)" The first five notes are a rockin' blues cliche that guitarists from Jimmy Page to Gary Moore carry in their hip pocket.

EX. 6

Ex. 7 is based on a Van Halen lick from "Right Now." No doubt Eddie was inspired by Chuck Berry for this one. Keep the first finger barre on the double-stops F♯ and C♯ while bending B notes with your 3rd finger. Using this pattern, move up eight frets to the 10th fret, and you will then be in the same key (F Maj. Pent) as the original lick.

EX. 7

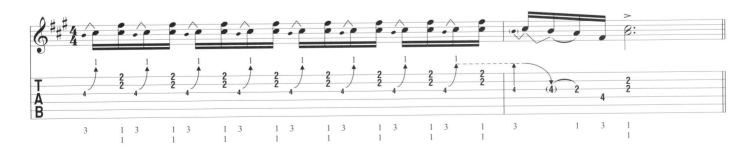

At the beginning of this section, you will see a diagram of frets 1–5 with two notes played on each string. The fingering shown is played in 2nd position. 2nd position simply means your first finger is positioned over the 2nd fret. This pattern of notes is where you (and Van Halen, Nuno, Schenker, etc.) got these riffs from. The pattern is made up of five notes, A, B, C♯, E, F♯ (the A Major Pentatonic Scale), that are repeatedly found throughout the neck. Every riff you play in this chapter will be made up of these same five notes. In fact, Ex. 5 is made up of all but one note of the pattern we've explored in this area of the neck. Check the examples to see that they come from Pattern 1 (which, as shown in the diagram, starts on the note F♯ of the low E string). Now experiment yourself, using any order and combination of notes from Pattern 1. Try playing each of the two notes per string using only pull-offs or hammer-ons.

> *I didn't really study blues. But when I first started soloing, those were just the simplest, easiest notes there to hit. When I stumbled onto it, I said, "Hey this is what they're doing in the blues. Great, I know those notes." I just kind of expanded from there.*
>
> —Eddie Van Halen (Van Halen)

PATTERN 2

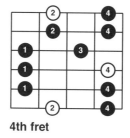

4th fret

Ex. 8 is the kind of repeated riff used in Lynyrd Skynyrd's "Free Bird."

EX. 8

Ex. 9 was inspired by Booker T & the M.G.'s, with the classic rock guitar playing of Steve Cropper.

EX. 8

Ex. 10 has its roots in the Boston song "Long Time." Using this pattern, move up eight frets to the 12th fret, and you will be in the same key (F Maj. Pent.) as the original lick.

EX. 10

Ex. 11 is based on a lick from Queen's "Tie Your Mother Down," which is also played in the same key we are using.

EX. 11

Ex. 12 is a variation of a lick from "Song of the Wind." Notice how Santana's last note in the first bar serves as a pickup for the second phrase in bar two. Phrasing over the bar is one of many elements that help define a player's style.

EX. 12

Ex. 13 is the exact same riff as Ex. 1, just played in a different position on the neck. The point is to show you that all of the Pentatonic riffs presented in this book, as well as those you make up yourself, can be played in different patterns, and occasionally different octaves, throughout the entire length of the neck.

EX. 13

Ex. 14 is a descending lick that is similar to something that Dickie Betts played in The Allman Brothers' tune "Jessica." Besides its musicality, this line also happens to include every note in Pattern 2. Using this pattern, move up five frets to the 10th fret, and you will be in the same key (D Major Pentatonic) as the original lick.

EX. 14

At the beginning of this section you will see a diagram of the strings for frets 4–7 (4th position). Once again, we've got two notes played per string. And you'll notice that the notes in Ex. 8–14 can be found in Pattern 2, as seen in the diagram. Now invent your own riffs using the notes in Pattern 2 (which starts on the note A of the low E string).

> *B.B. King will play one note and it will sing and have a purity about it that says so much. If any guitar player has that kind of thing in him, that feel that comes across in the course of one note, then you know they're on the right track.*
> *—John Mayall (Blues Breakers)*

PATTERN 3

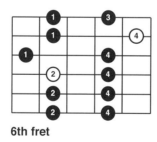

6th fret

Ex. 15, as country as it sounds, has its roots in the Guns N' Roses song, "Used to Love Her."

EX. 15

Ex. 16 may remind you of Lenny Kravitz in "Are You Gonna Go My Way." Using this same pattern, move up eight frets to the 14th fret, and you can jam along with Lenny.

EX. 16

Ex. 17 is a Tesla-inspired lick that could have come from "Love Song." You'll notice some pull-offs and hammer-ons are done with your 4th finger. Building strength in a weaker finger is one of the best things you can do for your technique. Using this same pattern, move down two frets to the 4th fret, and you will then be in the same key as Tesla.

EX. 17

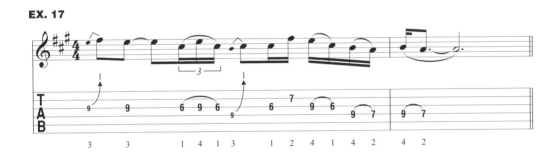

Ex.'s 18 and 19 find us once again going back to Santana's *Caravanserai* recording for more ideas inspired by "Song of the Wind."

EX. 18

EX. 19

Ex. 20 is inspired by several players and songs, including Eric Johnson's signature tune, "Cliffs of Dover." Tab readers should think of each set of three notes (a triplet) as one beat. This will help give swing to the riff. Play this one smoothly, and when you bring it up to speed, you've got a ripper.

EX. 20

At the beginning of this section, you will see a diagram of the strings for frets 6–10 (6th position). Again, there are two notes played per string, and Ex. 15–20 can be found in Pattern 3, as seen in the diagram. Check to see that this is true, and then experiment with your own licks in this 3rd pattern (which starts on the B note of the low E string).

> *Most of your blues guitar players aren't schooled players. They just play Pentatonic Major and Minor scales. It takes them a long way.*
> —Ernie C (Body Count)

PATTERN 4

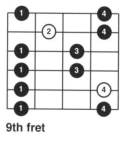

9th fret

Ex. 21 is a variation of a lick from "Statesboro Blues" by The Allman Brothers.

EX. 21

Ex. 22 is similar to a Leslie West lick from Mountain's "Mississippi Queen." Using this pattern, move up seven frets to the 19th fret, and you can play along with Leslie in E Major Pentatonic.

EX. 22

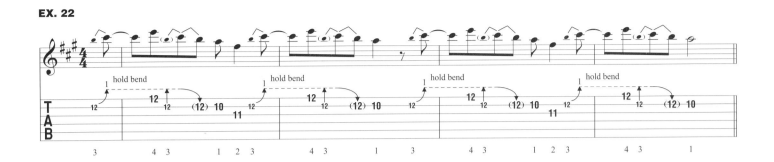

Ex. 23 is similar to the opening solo lick in "Blue Sky" by The Allman Brothers Band.

EX. 23

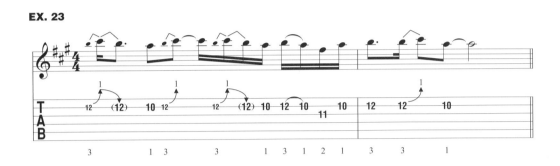

Ex. 24 has two inspired bits put together. The first bar is one of "The" classic B.B. King licks. The rest of the lick is along the lines of a Johnny Winter bit, played in "Be Careful with a Fool." If you want to rock out with Johnny, move this lick up three frets to the key of C Major Pentatonic.

EX. 24

Ex. 25 has its roots in a line from Boston's "Peace of Mind." Using this pattern, move up seven frets to the 16th fret or move down five frets to the 4th fret, and you will be in the same key (E Major Pentatonic) as the original lick.

EX. 25

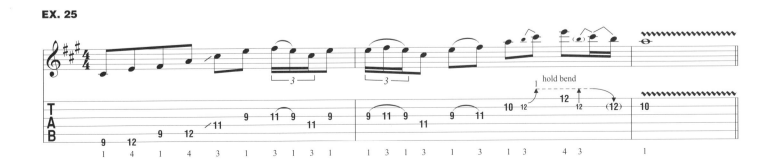

Ex. 26 is based on a line from The Allman Brothers' instrumental "Jessica."

EX. 26

Ex. 27 is a scale exercise in Pattern 4, common to a lot of rock music. Keep in mind that you can play this exercise in any of the patterns.

EX. 27

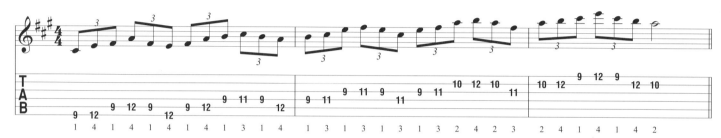

At the start of this section, you will see a diagram of the strings from frets 9–12 (9th position). By now, I'm sure you've guessed that we're playing two notes per string and that every note in Ex. 21–27 can be found in Pattern 4, as seen in the diagram. Verify this for yourself, and then explore your own ideas in this 4th pattern (which starts on the C♯ note of the low E string).

> *Blues is the most emotional form of guitar playing I can think of It's about choice of notes and vibrato, never speed. That's why the greatest players have never been the fastest players. They have always been the guys who chose the notes. Clapton said it best when he said, "It's not what you put into your solo, it's what you leave out that makes a great solo."*
>
> —Gene Simmons (Kiss)

PATTERN 5

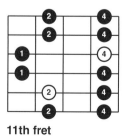

11th fret

Ex. 28 starts as a variation of a solo lick from Led Zeppelin's "What Is and What Should Never Be," and finishes with a classic blues ending.

EX. 28

Ex. 29 is in the style of an ascending and descending line from Eric Johnson's "Righteous."

EX. 29

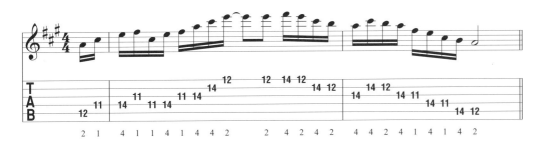

Ex. 30 sounds like a line from "Alex Chilton" by The Replacements, which is also played in the same key we are using here.

EX. 30

Ex. 31 is similar to a lick from Tesla's "Love Song." Using this same pattern, move down two frets to the 9th fret, and you will be in the same key as Tesla's original.

EX. 31

Ex. 32 is the exact same riff as Ex. 24. It's another example of how a riff in one pattern, or area of the neck, will also work in another. All you need to do is duplicate the notes.

EX. 32

At the start of this section, you will see a diagram of the strings from frets 11–14 (11th position). We're playing two notes per string, and every riff in Ex. 28–32 can be found in Pattern 5, as seen in the diagrams. Check to be certain and then make up your own riffs in this 5th pattern (which starts on the E note of the low E string).

> *I practiced more than people my age when I was 13 or 14, and all I wanted to do was play out.*
>
> —Blues Saraceno

COMBINING PATTERNS

Now that you are familiar with the five positions on the neck where A Major Pentatonic licks can be played, it becomes crucial that you start combining the patterns. The most common pitfall a guitarist faces when first exploring the Major Pentatonic scales is the tendency to play in one position, particularly Pattern 1.

Ex. 33 is a take on an Eric Johnson lick from "Righteous," using Patterns 1, 2, and 3. Notice that your switch to the next pattern is made by sliding up a note.

EX. 33

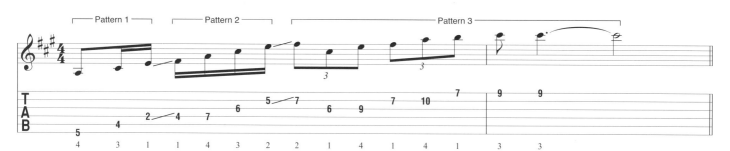

Ex. 34 is a descending figure similar to what The Grateful Dead's Jerry Garcia might play. It starts with Pattern 3, and slides down through Pattern 2 on the way to Pattern 1.

EX. 34

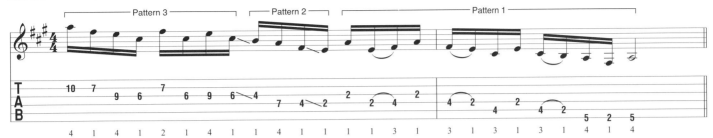

Ex. 35 is an exercise that goes through all the patterns numerically, starting with 1. You can use the exercise in combinations of any two strings you like! This is a good test to show you how well you actually know the patterns throughout the entire neck.

EX. 35

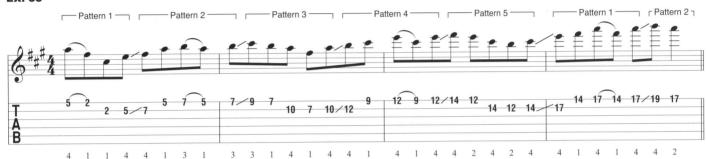

Ex. 36 is a descending line inspired by Stevie Ray Vaughan. You'll notice that it goes through four of the five patterns. Using this riff, move down six frets, to the 11th fret and you will be in the same key (E♭ Major Pentatonic) as the original lick, or as Stevie Ray Vaughan generally does, you can tune down a half step and start the lick at the 12th fret and play with him.

EX. 36

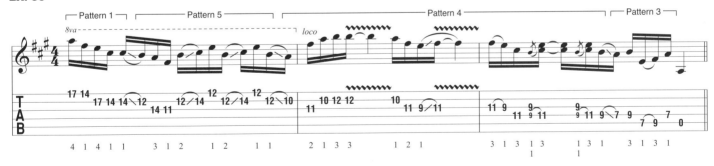

Ex.37 is a Jimmy Page-inspired lick from "The Song Remains the Same." Here we utilize Patterns 1–4.

EX. 37

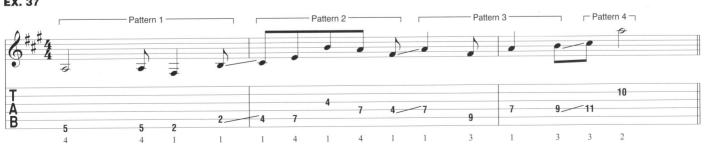

SOLO

Ex. 38 is a solo that contains some of the licks presented in this book. Above the musical notation, you will see Roman numerals that tell you what position to play in. The solo starts in 10th position. Do you recognize which pattern it starts on? As you play through the solo, stop to recognize the patterns as you move through them.

The vocabulary of guitar masters like Clapton, Hendrix, and Van Halen is yours to explore. The notes they play are the same notes you play. How you make them speak is the essence of style—both yours and theirs. The only limit is your own imagination. Remember that the tab, fingerings, and phrasing (hammer-ons, slides, vibrato, etc.) are merely suggestions, a place to start. Take these ideas, play around with them, and turn them into your own voice.

EX. 38

Solo Notes:

- The opening pickup lick was inspired by The Grateful Dead's "Truckin."
- Meas. 2, 6 and 12 incorporate standard blues/rock licks that can be found in songs as diverse as The Allman Brothers, "One Way Out," Queen's "Tie Your Mother Down," and Toto's "Rosanna."
- Meas. 3 has two sextuplets, which may remind you of the playing of Steve Morse or George Benson.

CHORD PROGRESSIONS

Ex. 39–42 show four chord progressions you can improvise over while using any of the licks and scale patterns you've learned in this book. There are many chords to play A Major Pentatonic over. Some of the most popular chords are A, A7, A⁶, Amaj7, F#m, and F#m7. Just as useful, but somewhat less popular, are Bm, Bm7, Bm11, B9sus4, C#m, C#m7, D, Dmaj9, D⁶, E, and E7. Mix and match these chords in any order you like, and make up your own progressions and songs. Ex. 42 can be used as the backing track for the solo in Ex. 38.

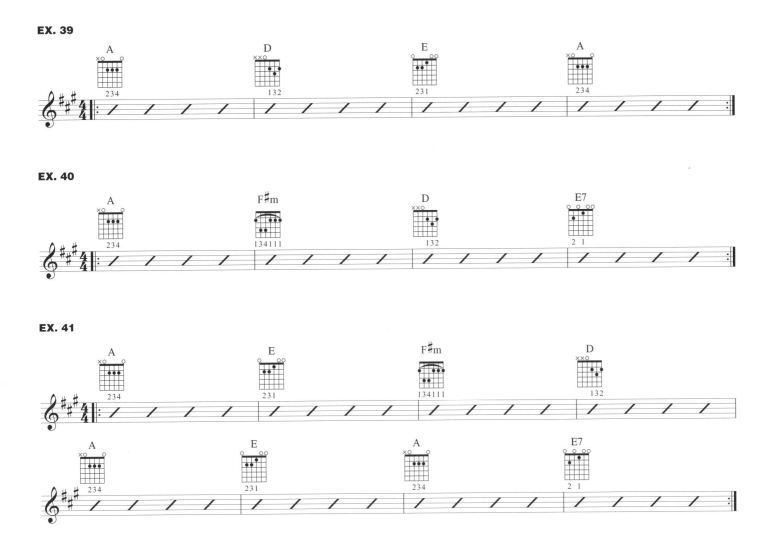

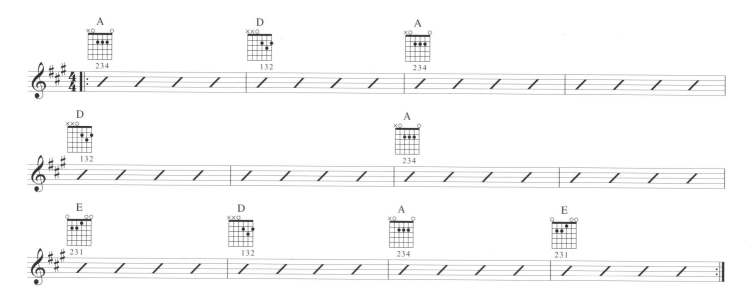

ABOUT THE A MAJOR PENTATONIC SCALE

The A Major Pentatonic Scale consists of five notes from the A Major Scale (A, B, C♯, D, E, F♯, G♯). These notes are: A (Root), B (2nd), C♯ (3rd), E (5th), and F♯ (6th).

Although many possibilities exist, the five basic patterns presented in this book are the most commonly and widely used for playing these notes systematically on the guitar. As you recognize and practice each pattern presented together on the neck, in the following diagram, and in notation and tablature, be aware of where the root notes (A) lie in the patterns so that you will be able to play these patterns (transpose them) in other keys.

Referring to the following diagram, some of you may also notice an easy way to find the five notes of ANY Major Pentatonic Scale. In this case, start with the A root on any string, and play six sequential notes with the last note being the root note (A) an octave away. These notes happen to make up the bass line to "My Girl" by The Temptations. You can use this signature riff, in addition to the diagrams, to help you find the Major Pentatonic Scale all over the neck. For Major Pentatonic Scales other than A, do the same thing, only change the root or starting note.

5 BASIC PATTERNS OF THE
A MAJOR PENTATONIC SCALE

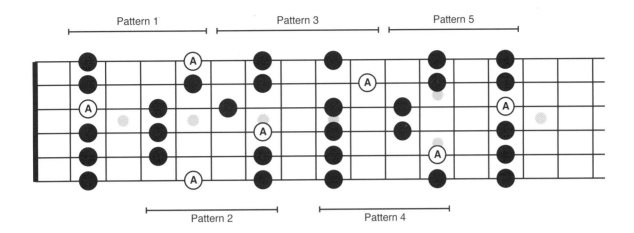

The diagram above shows you all of the A Major Pentatonic notes on the neck; the individual patterns are noted by the brackets above and below the diagram. Notice the overlapping or common notes and how they are shared by consecutive patterns. Using this diagram you can invent your own patterns by, for example, playing three notes per string.

Pattern 1

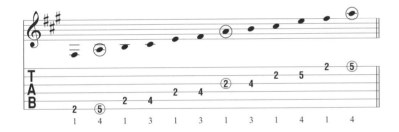

Pattern 2

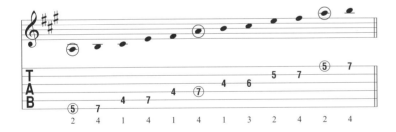

Pattern 3

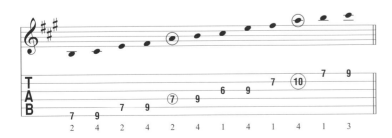

Pattern 4

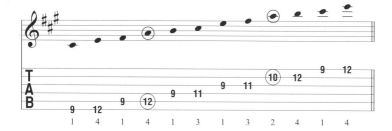

Pattern 5

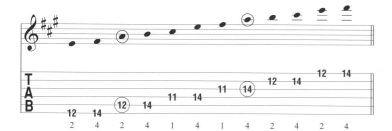

> The problem I had when I started playing guitar solos was that I was stuck in a box. I knew this one position of the scale and I tended to stay there.
> —Alex Skolnick (Testament, Exhibit A)

> The heart of what I do as a lead player is the blues. But with no rules attached. I'm not going to stick with any of it because it feels like it ought to be there.
> —David Gilmour (Pink Floyd)

TRANSPOSING

The example below is a repeat of Ex. 7, presented in Pattern 1, with our root note A on the E strings. But what if you want to play the same lick or pattern in E Major Pentatonic? Since your new root note, E, is located seven frets up from A, we simply move the same lick or pattern up seven frets, in this case to the 9th fret.

EX. 43

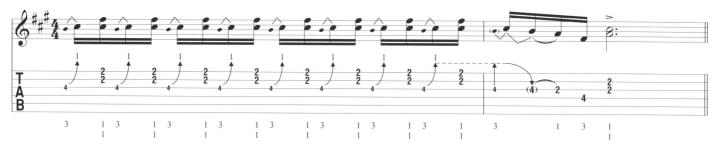

Ex. 44 is the exact same lick as Ex. 7, only now you're playing the lick transposed to E Major Pentatonic. This is one common way to transpose. Pick a lick from ANY of the A Major Pentatonic patterns and move it up seven frets. Play it exactly the same and you're playing in E Major Pentatonic. Pick another A Major Pentatonic lick from anywhere on the neck, but this time move up three frets. Now you are playing it in C Major Pentatonic. Why? Because the new root note, C, is located three frets away from A. Pick any lick in A Major Pentatonic, move it down two frets, and you're playing it in G Major Pentatonic.

EX. 44

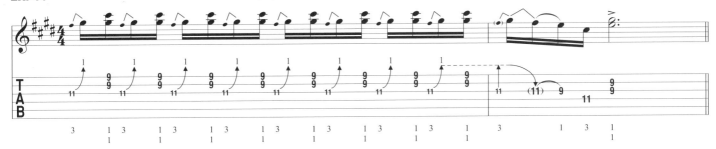

So if you want to transpose (move) a lick from the A Major Pentatonic Scale to another key, locate your new root note on either E string, or any string you choose. Count how many frets up or down it is from the original root note A, and move the riff up or down that same number of frets. Refer to the previous diagram (the patterns presented on the neck) to learn where the roots of each scale pattern can be found on all the strings. You may use a root note on any string to transpose. REMEMBER, THIS RULE ALWAYS WORKS!

The diagram below shows you how this rule works. You can see what it looks like when you transpose from the 2nd position A Major Pentatonic Scale to the 9th position E Major Pentatonic Scale.

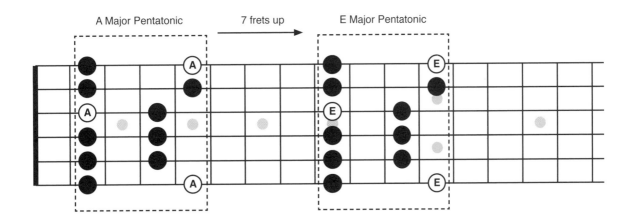

We've referred to all of the examples in this book as being in A Major Pentatonic. The A Major Pentatonic Scale (A, B, C♯, E, F♯) contains exactly the same notes as the F♯ Minor Pentatonic Scale (F♯, A, B, C♯, E). One is a relative scale of the other, meaning that the two share the same key signature and notes but have different roots and different orders of notes. The root of the relative minor scale is always three frets down or nine frets up from the root of its relative major scale. So when you are playing in A Major Pentatonic, you are also playing the notes in the F♯ Minor Pentatonic. It's one scale with two names! The difference in sounds will be made by which root note you start and end your lines on and which chords you play over. Looking over the examples in this chapter, you will see that, with rare exception, most of them end on the note A. Below is a list of Major Pentatonic Scales and their Relative Minor Pentatonic Scales.

Major	Minor	Major	Minor
C	Am	G♭(F♯)	E♭m(D♯m)
F	Dm	B	G♯m
B♭(A♯)	Gm	E	C♯m
E♭(D♯)	Cm	A	F♯m
A♭(G♯)	Fm	D	Bm
D♭(C♯)	B♭m(A♯m)	G	Em

To give yourself the widest range of Pentatonic possibilities for your songs and solos, you should learn to mix the Major Pentatonic and Minor Pentatonic Scales together. For while both scales can and do stand alone, they were tailor-made to combine with each other. If you are interested in learning more about this idea, check out the next chapter on Minor Pentatonic Scales for Guitar.

RECOMMENDED LISTENING

The following is a list of songs which utilize the Major Pentatonic Scale:

"A Lil' Ain't Enough" — David Lee Roth
"Alex Chilton" — The Replacements
"Are You Gonna Go My Way" — Lenny Kravitz
"Backwater" — Meat Puppets
"Be Careful With a Fool" — Johnny Winter
"Captain Nemo" — Michael Schenker
"Castles Made of Sand" — Jimi Hendrix
"Cliffs of Dover" — Eric Johnson
"Decadence Dance" — Extreme
"Deuce" — Kiss
"Free Bird" — Lynyrd Skynrd
"Go Your Own Way" — Fleetwood Mac
"Heartbreaker" — Led Zeppelin
"Hotel California" — Eagles
"I Love Rock and Roll" — Joan Jett
"Jealous Again" — Black Crowes
"Jeepster" — T-Rex
"Jessica" — The Allman Brothers Band
"Learning to Fly" — Pink Floyd
"Life Goes On" — Poison
"Lola" — Kinks
"Long Time" — Boston
"Love Song" — Tesla
"Miles Away" — Winger
"Mississippi Queen" — Mountain
"Mutha (Don't Wanna Go to School Today)" — Extreme
"My Old School" — Steely Dan
"One Way Out" — The Allman Brothers Band
"Peace of Mind" — Boston
"People Get Ready" — Jeff Beck
"Right Now" — Van Halen
"Righteous" — Eric Johnson
'Rosanna" — Toto
"Song of the Wind" — Santana
"Statesboro Blues" — The Allman Brothers Band
"Suffragette City" — David Bowie
"Tie Your Mother Down" — Queen
"Truckin'" — The Grateful Dead
"Used to Love Her" — Guns N' Roses
"Walk This Way" — Aerosmith
"What Is and What Should Never Be" — Led Zeppelin

Minor Pentatonic Scales

FOR GUITAR

INTRODUCTION

Pentatonic scales are the single most important building blocks for the rock guitar soloist. They are at the heart of all rock scales and the foundation upon which greats from Jimmy Page and Jimi Hendrix to Eddie Van Halen, Diamond Darrell and Eric Johnson have built their styles.

The word *Pentatonic* has Greek origins. *Penta* means five and *Tonic* means tone. So we've got five notes (or tones) that make up the Pentatonic scale. That's all you need to know for now. Just spend as much time as you need with the tablature explanation and let's play.

EXPLAINING TABLATURE

Tablature is a paint-by-number language telling you which notes to play on the fingerboard. Each of the six lines represents a string on the guitar. The numbers on the line indicate which frets to press down. Note that tablature does not indicate the rhythm.

NOTATION LEGEND

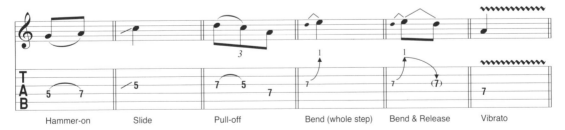

| Hammer-on | Slide | Pull-off | Bend (whole step) | Bend & Release | Vibrato |

Hammer-on:

Pick the first (lower) note, then "hammer on" to sound the higher note with another finger by fretting it without picking.

Slide:

Strike the first note, and then, without striking it again, use the same left-hand finger to slide up or down the string to the second note.

Pull-off:

Place both fingers on the notes to be sounded. Pick the first (higher) note, then sound the lower note by "pulling off" the finger on the higher note while keeping the lower note fretted.

Bend (whole step):

Pick the note and bend up a whole step (two frets).

Bend & Release:

Pick the note and bend up a whole step, then release the bend back to the original note. All three notes are tied together; only the first note is attacked.

Vibrato:

Vibrate the note by rapidly bending and releasing the string using a left-hand finger, wrist, or forearm.

Finger Number:

Suggested fingerings are included under the tab staff for all examples. However, you should experiment with different fingerings and play the one that feels most comfortable to you.

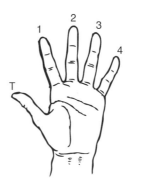

T = thumb
1 = 1st finger
2 = 2nd finger
3 = 3rd finger
4 = 4th finger

All examples in this book are presented in the A Minor Pentatonic Scale. Practice each lick very slowly, until you can play them very smoothly. Play a cool lick sloppily and people will hear the slop, not the lick.

Before you dive into the A Minor Pentatonic Scale, we offer this sound advice from some guitarists who got there first:

Rock 'n' roll is our folk music today. It's people getting together and listening, and getting into a common thing. That's what folk music is. The real blues is sitting around your porch with friends and jamming.

—Joe Perry (Aerosmith)

I discover new things by building a hot rod. I have to have that other foil and that challenge. I get dizzy building a rod because it's so thrilling. There's physical action there. You burn your fingers, there's grinding and welding. My garage is my playroom. There is rhythm all around a workshop. Music is everywhere. If I do a certain quota of that a week I keep my brain together. Then I come and practice. But I couldn't sit in a room and just practice the guitar. Nothing would come out.

—Jeff Beck

Playing naturally and off the cuff is cool. But you have to practice a certain amount to get there. If you don't try stuff, you don't know to what extent you can learn from it. You have to do a certain amount of practicing to discover new feeling. You're not born with everything you end up with. You learn a lot along the way.

—Michael Fath

PATTERN 1

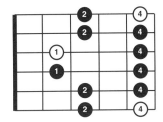

Ex. 1 is a variation of a hammer-on lick that Eric Clapton played on Freddie King's classic instrumental, "Hideaway." Using this pattern, move up seven frets to the 10th fret. You will be in the same key as the original recording—and you can play along with the Blues Breakers! At the end of this chapter is a simple explanation of how you can take our examples presented in A Minor Pentatonic and easily transpose them to different keys; in this case, E Minor Pentatonic.

EX. 1

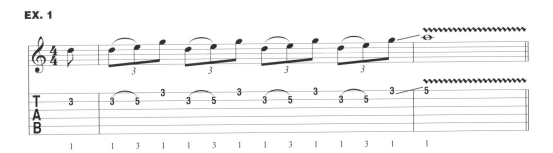

Ex. 2 was inspired by Joe Satriani's "Satch Boogie," which is also played in the same key we are using here. Use this suggested fingering, or start the riff with your 3rd finger and see how it falls on your fretting hand. The last descending line may remind you of the main Hendrix riff on "I Don't Live Today."

EX. 2

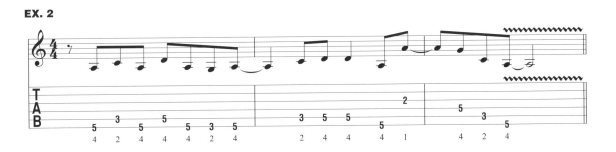

Ex. 3 is an ascending sequence in triplet, reminiscent of what Jimmy Page did in Led Zeppelin's "Good Times Bad Times." He also used the same key we are using here. There's a similar run in the tune "Don't Want You No More" by the Allman Brothers.

EX. 3

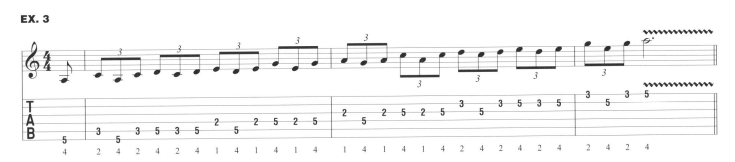

Ex. 4 is a lick à la Eric Clapton from his Blues Breakers version of "Steppin' Out." Move up ten frets to the 12th fret and you will be in the same key as the original recording.

EX. 4

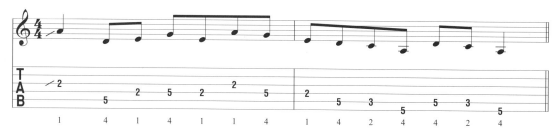

At the top of this section you see a diagram of frets 1–5 with two notes played on each string. The fingering shown is played in 2nd position. 2nd position simply means your first finger is positioned over the 2nd fret. This pattern of notes is where you (and Clapton, Page, Satriani, etc.) got these riffs from. The pattern is made up of five notes, A, C, D, E, G (the A Minor Pentatonic Scale) that are repeatedly found throughout the neck. Every riff you play in this chapter will be made up of these same five notes. In fact Ex. 3 is made up of all but one note of the pattern we've explored in this area of the neck. Check the examples to see that they come from Pattern 1 (which, as shown above, starts on the note G of the low E string). Now experiment yourself using any order and combination of notes from Pattern 1. Try playing each of the two notes per string using only pull-offs or hammer-ons.

> When I was 13 I copied Hendrix, Clapton, Jimmy Page, and Jeff Beck—those were the guys that were my idols. Those were the guys that were doing the best rock riffs around.
>
> —Ace Frehley (Kiss)

PATTERN 2

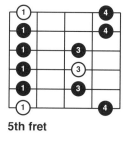

5th fret

Ex. 5 may remind you of a riff from Zeppelin's "Stairway to Heaven," which was also played in the same key we are using.

EX. 5

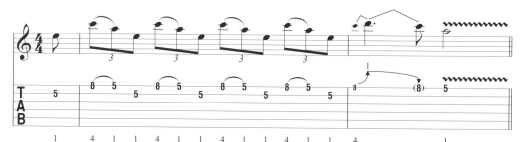

Ex. 6 was inspired by Led Zeppelin's "Black Dog," also originally written in the same key we are playing here. Make sure to bend the D note a whole step (two frets) up to E. This is a classic rock riff used by just about everybody who has ever plugged into a Marshall stack.

EX. 6

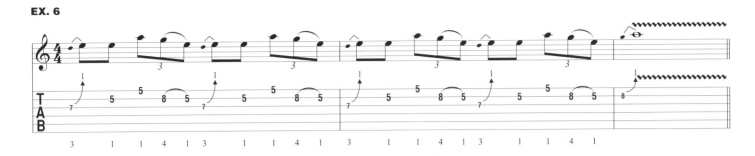

Ex. 7 is a descending triplet sequence using pull-offs. The idea is similar to Ex. 3, only it's going down the scale instead of up.

EX. 7

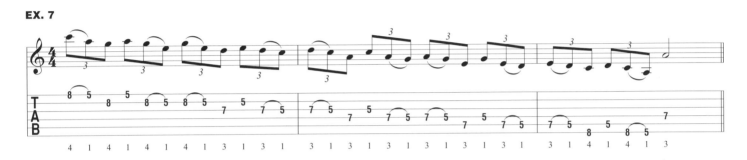

Ex. 8 is similar to a riff heard on Cream's version of "Crossroads," which is also played in the same key we are using.

EX. 8

Ex. 9 is the exact same riff as Ex. 4. The point is to show you that all of the Pentatonic riffs presented in this book, and all those you make up yourself, can be played in different patterns, occasionally different octaves, throughout the entire length of the neck.

EX. 9

At the beginning of this section you will see a diagram of the strings for frets 5–8 (5th position). Once again we've got two notes played per string. And you'll notice that the notes in Ex. 5–9 can be found in Pattern 2, as seen in the diagram. Now invent your own riffs using the notes in this Pattern 2 (which starts on the note A of the low E string).

PATTERN 3

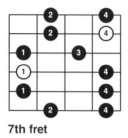

7th fret

Ex. 10 has its roots in John Lee Hooker's classic riff from "Boom Boom," which has been covered by artists ranging from Bruce Springsteen to Johnny Gale. Using this pattern, move down five frets to the 2nd fret, and you will be in the same key as the Animals' version.

EX. 10

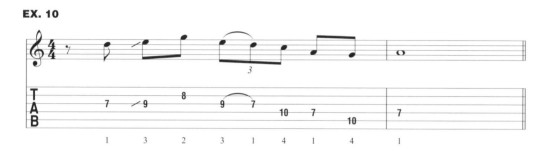

Ex. 11 may remind you of Angus Young in "Back In Black." Using this same pattern, move down five frets to the 2nd fret and you can jam with AC/DC.

EX. 11

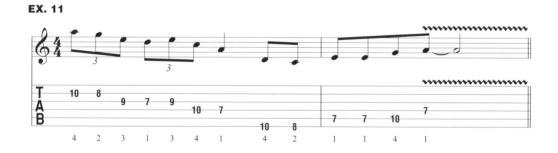

Ex. 12 is a Gary Moore-inspired lick that could have come from "Since I Met You Baby." Using this same pattern, move up three frets to the 11th fret and you will be in the same key as Gary.

EX. 12

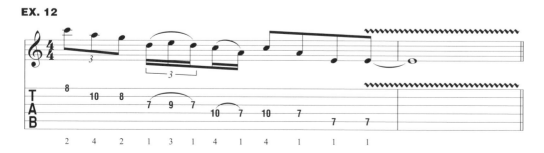

Ex. 13 is again inspired by Zeppelin's "Black Dog." Tab readers should think of notes 3–5 as one beat (triplet) and notes 6–8 as one beat (triplet). This will help give swing to the riff.

EX. 13

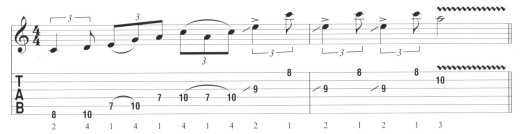

Ex. 14 is the exact same riff as Ex. 7. It's another example of how a riff in one pattern, or area of the neck, will also work in another. All you need to do is duplicate the notes.

EX. 14

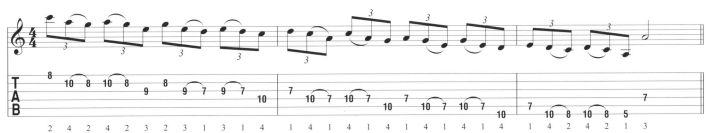

At the beginning of this section you will see a diagram of the strings for frets 7–10 (7th position). Again there are two notes played per string and Ex. 10–14 can be found in Pattern 3 as seen in the diagram. Check to see that this is true and then experiment with your own licks in this 3rd pattern (which starts on the note C of the low E string).

> *I thought I had a lot of licks down, and I pulled out some Johnny Winter albums that I've been listening to for years. I heard another 500 riffs that I don't have down. It's the feeling and little pauses and hesitations I have to study. From one blues record, you can learn for years.*
>
> —Tom Keifer (Cinderella)

PATTERN 4

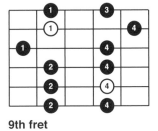

9th fret

Ex. 15 is a variation of a lick from "All Your Love" by Eric Clapton with the Blues Breakers, which is also played in the same key we are using.

EX. 15

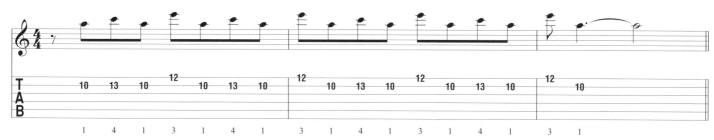

Ex. 16 is similar to another Clapton lick, this time from "Crossroads," which is also played in the same key we are using.

EX. 16

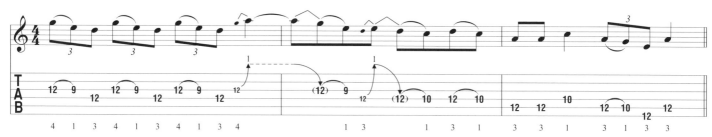

Ex. 17 is similar to the opening solo lick in "Crossroads." Because there are so few notes, it's Eric Clapton's phrasing that makes this lick memorable.

EX. 17

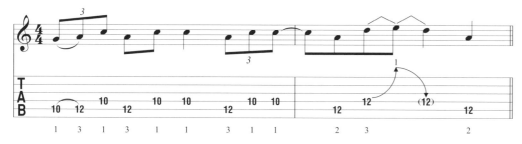

Ex. 18 was inspired by a Beatles lick from "The End," which was also played in the same key we are using here.

EX. 18

> *I can only tell you that I know for a fact one scale. I know the box scale, the pentatonic. You can play it anyplace.*
>
> —*Kerry King (Slayer)*

Ex. 19 is the exact same riff as Ex. 10. Again we see how riffs are universal in all patterns. Notice in this case that the pulls-offs are on different strings.

EX. 19

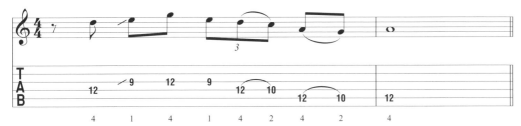

At the beginning of this section you will see a diagram of the strings from frets 9–13 (9th position). By now I'm sure you've guessed that we're playing two notes per string and that every note in Ex. 15–19 can be found in Pattern 4, as seen in the diagram. Verify this for yourself and then explore your own ideas in this 4th pattern (which starts on the D note of the low E string).

PATTERN 5

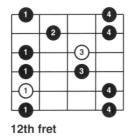

12th fret

Ex. 20 is a variation of a lick from Cream's "Strange Brew," originally played in the same key we are using here.

EX. 20

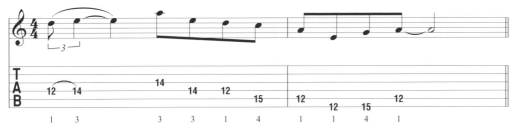

Ex. 21 is inspired by Lenny Kravitz's hit "Are You Gonna Go My Way." Using this same pattern, move down five frets to the 10th fret, and you can play along with Lenny.

EX. 21

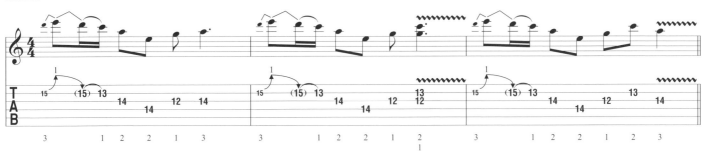

Ex. 22 sounds like a line from "Crossroads."

EX. 22

Ex. 23 is similar to a lick from "Hideaway." Using this same pattern, move down five frets to the 7th fret and you will be in the same key as the original.

EX. 23

Ex. 24 is the exact same riff as Ex. 15. Again we hammer the point that a riff you learn in one pattern is easily duplicated all over the neck, just by playing the same notes.

EX. 24

At the start of this section you will see a diagram of the strings from frets 12–15 (12th position). We're playing two notes per string and every note from every riff in Ex. 20–24 can be found in this Pattern 5, as seen in the diagram. Check to be certain, and then make up your own riffs in this 5th pattern (which starts on the E note of the low E string).

> *I ran into pentatonic scales and figured them out. Since they fall so comfortably on the guitar, I started improvising probably before I even knew what I was doing.*
>
> —Greg Howe

COMBINING PATTERNS

Now that you are familiar with the five positions on the neck where A Minor Pentatonic licks can be played, it becomes crucial that you start combining the patterns. The most common pitfall a guitarist faces when first exploring the Pentatonic scales is the tendency to play in one position, particularly Pattern 2.

Ex. 25 is a variation of a lick from "Black Dog" using Patterns 1 and 2.

EX. 25

Ex. 26 is a combination of ascending and descending triplet figures using Patterns 2 and 3.

EX. 26

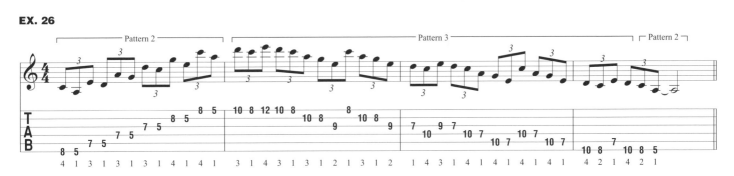

Ex. 27 is a repeating pull-off lick. The first note of every two sextuplets moves up scale-wise, A, C, D, E, G, as the lick moves through all the patterns.

EX. 27

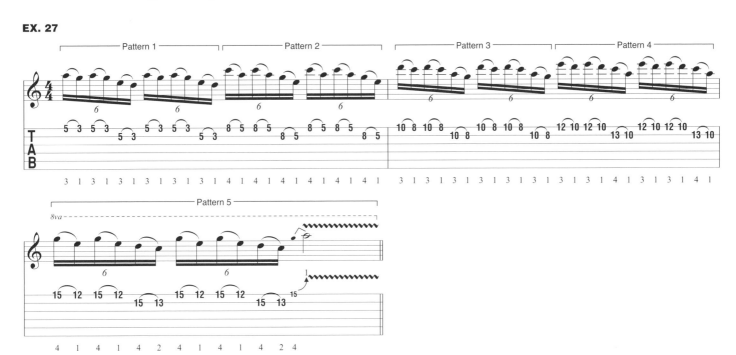

Ex. 28 is a Johnny Winter-inspired lick. The transition from one pattern to the next moves up scale-wise (starting on C) as the lick moves through all the patterns.

EX. 28

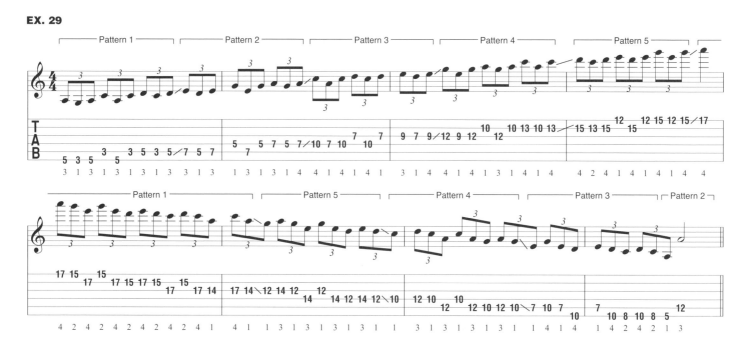

Ex. 29 is made up of ascending and descending triplets that cover all the positions shown in this book. You'll notice that after every three triplets there is a slide to the next pattern. Try changing patterns after only two triplets, or perhaps four. There are so many different ways and fingerings you can use to connect the patterns. You do yourself a disservice if you only play this example as shown. And remember to start slowly. Never build up your speed at the expense of playing smoothly.

EX. 29

CHORD PROGRESSIONS

Ex. 30–33 show four chord progressions you can improvise over while using any of the licks and scale patterns you've learned in this book. There are many chords to play A Minor Pentatonic over. Some of the most popular chords used in rock music are A, A7, Am, C, Cmaj7, Dm, Dm7, Em, Em7, F, G and G7. Mix and match these chords in any order you like and make up your own progressions and songs. Ex. 33 can be used as the backing track for the solo in Ex. 34.

EX. 30

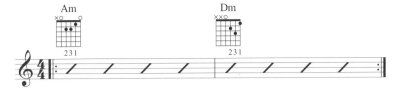

EX. 31

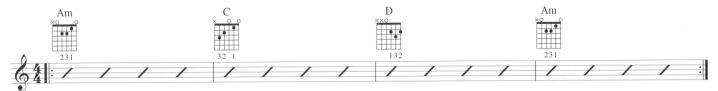

EX. 32

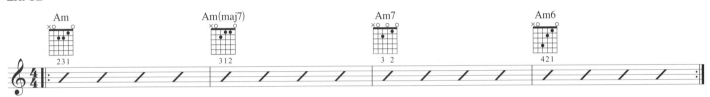

EX. 33

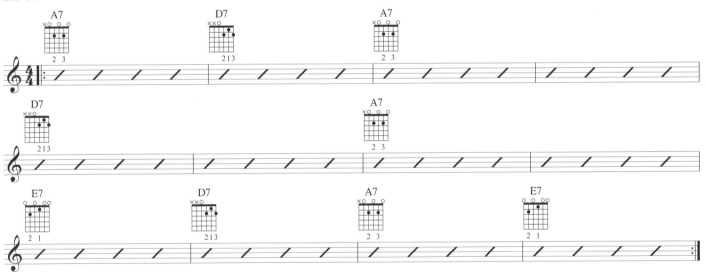

> *When you practice, you pick up ideas and chord changes that are good for leads, ideas that you want to find a way into the song.*
> —Glenn Tipton (Judas Priest)

> *Instead of thinking in terms of notes, I think in terms of sentences. I think of three-or four-bar phrases. It makes it easier for me that way. When we talk we are not thinking about every word we say, we are thinking about the idea of the sentence.*
> —Drew Zingg (Steely Dan)

SOLO

Ex. 34 is a solo using all of the areas/patterns on the fingerboard, incorporating some of the licks presented in this chapter. Above the musical notation you will see Roman numerals that tell you what positions to play in. The solo starts in 5th position. Do you recognize which pattern it starts on? As you play through the solo, stop to recognize the patterns as you move through them.

This solo is one of the endless possibilities available to you. The only limit is your own imagination. Stevie Ray Vaughan, Mike McCready and Joe Perry use these same notes and patterns. What makes each guitarist different is how they put them together. Remember that the TAB, fingerings and phrasing (hammer-ons, slides, vibrato, etc.) are merely suggestions, a place to start. Take these ideas and play them with your own voice.

EX. 34

Solo Notes:

- The opening pickup lick was used by The Allman Brothers on "Statesboro Blues."
- Meas. 2–3 use Ex. 11 extended over two octaves.
- Meas. 4 is a quote from Ex. 13.
- Meas. 7 and 8 use the familiar blues lick found in Ex. 6.
- Meas. 9–11 are a variation and sequence based on Ex. 7.
- Meas. 12 is based on Ex. 3.

ABOUT THE A MINOR PENTATONIC SCALE

The A Minor Penatonic Scale consists of five notes from the A Natural Minor Scale (A,B,C,D,E,F,G). These notes are: A (Root) C (♭3rd) D (4th) E (5th) and G (♭7th).

Although many possibilities exist, the five basic patterns presented in this book are commonly and widely used for playing these notes systematically on the guitar. As you recognize and practice each pattern presented together on the neck, in the diagram below, and in notation and tablature, be aware of where the root notes lie in the patterns, so you will be able to play these patterns (transpose them) in other keys.

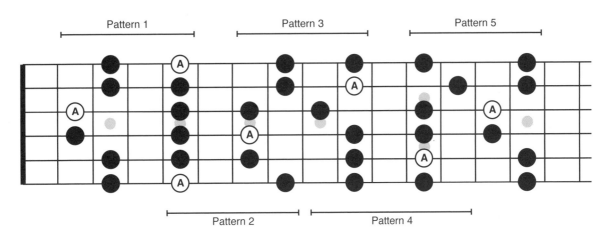

Pattern 1

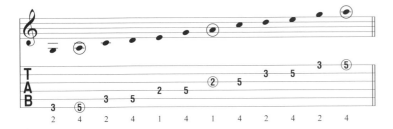

Pattern 2

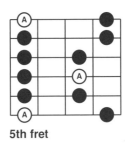

5th fret

Pattern 3

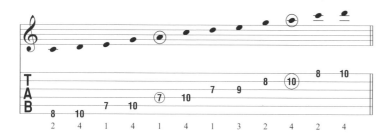
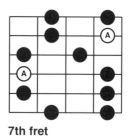

7th fret

Pattern 4

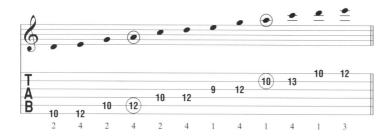
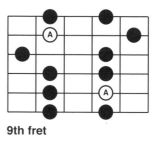

9th fret

Pattern 5

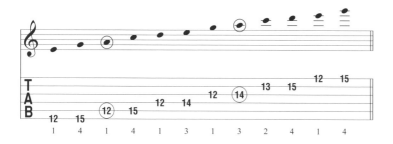
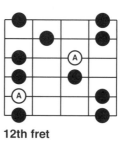

12th fret

TRANSPOSING

The example below is a repeat of Ex. 5, presented in Pattern 2, with the root note A on the E strings. But what if you want to play the same lick or pattern in D Minor Pentatonic? Since your new root note, D, is located five frets up from A, we simply move the same lick or pattern up five frets, in this case to the 10th fret.

EX. 35

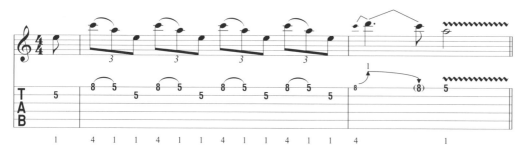

Ex. 36 is the exact same lick as Ex. 35, only now you're playing the lick transposed to D Minor Pentatonic. This is one common way to transpose. Pick a lick from any of the A Minor Pentatonic patterns and move it up five frets. Play it exactly the same and you're playing in D Minor Pentatonic. Pick another A Minor Pentatonic lick from anywhere on the neck, but this time move up three frets. Now you are playing in C Minor Pentatonic. Why? Because the new root note, C, is located three frets away from A. Pick any lick in A Minor Pentatonic, move it down two frets and you're playing it in G Minor Pentatonic.

EX. 36

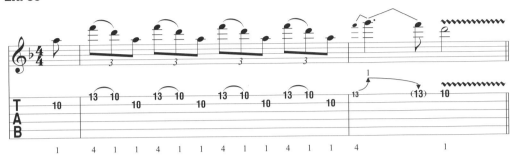

So if you want to transpose (move) a lick from the A Minor Pentatonic Scale to another key, locate your new root note on either E string, or any string you choose. Count how many frets up or down it is from the original root note A, and move the riff up or down that same number of frets. Refer to the previous diagram (the patterns presented on the neck) to learn where the roots of each scale pattern can be found on all the strings. You may use a root note on any string to transpose. Remember, this rule always works!

The diagram below shows you how this rule works. You can see what it looks like when you transpose from the 5th position A Minor Pentatonic Scale to the 10th position D Minor Pentatonic Scale.

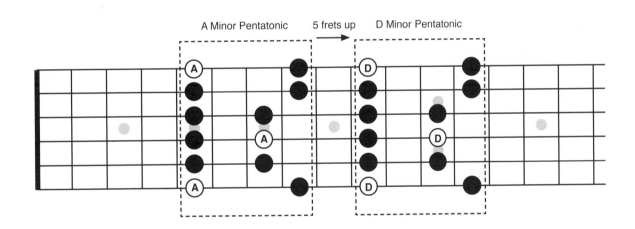

We've referred to all of the examples in this book as being in A Minor Pentatonic. The A Minor Pentatonic Scale (A C D E G) contains exactly the same notes as the C Major Pentatonic Scale (C D E G A); that's why they call them relative minor and relative major scales. The root of the relative minor scale is always three frets down or nine frets up from the root of its relative major scale. So when you are playing in A Minor Pentatonic, you are also playing the notes in the C Major Pentatonic. It's one scale with two names! The difference in sounds will be made by which root note you start and end your lines on and which chords you play over. If you are interested in learning more about this idea, check out the chapter on the Major Pentatonic Scale for Guitar.

> *Being able to play an instrument doesn't mean you know the scales and doesn't mean you have been taught the particular technique or style. Being able to play an instrument is being able to make music with it and having yourself be connected to the instrument, intimately enough that you can express whatever you want to.*
>
> —Kim Thayil (Soundgarden)

Modes for Rock & Blues GUITAR

INTRODUCTION

Very often, modes are to a self-taught rock guitarist what garlic is to a vampire. It's not life threatening, but it's scary. Yet modes have been used as a source of melody since the Middle Ages, perhaps as long as garlic has been used for medicinal purposes (for all but vampires), and centuries before anybody took up rock guitar playing. And although up until the '70s, the approach to rock guitar soloing had been almost exclusively to use blues and pentatonic scales, the influence of jazz and classical music has popularized the use of some modes in rock tunes, from Ozzy Osbourne's "Mr. Crowley" to R.E.M.'s "I Remember California." Their knowledge of modes has helped shape the individual styles of guitarists like Kirk Hammett, Yngwie Malmsteen, Joe Satriani, and John Petrucci.

In this book, you will see that the mode is not a complex idea at all; in fact, you may lose all fear of the modes once you realize that one way to look at them is as an altered Chuck Berry pentatonic "box scale!" We'll take each mode one step at a time, show what it is, where it comes from, how we can look at it in different ways, and how you can use it musically. You will also find musical examples in the style of various rock guitarists to help you play and recognize the sound of each mode, as well as some chord progressions to help you jam on your own. Hopefully, *Modes for Rock and Blues Guitar* will correct any misconception about the topic and will give you a good, solid understanding of modes and how to use them to enrich your own playing style.

> Sometimes, before I knew about modes, I would get caught in certain positions for certain keys and I wouldn't know I could go here and there. One thing that modes can do is get you familiar with the fretboard and you start seeing every key everywhere. Sometimes it gives you inspiration for new ideas. It can help you to bring out something you might not have done.
>
> —Greg Howe

EXPLAINING TABLATURE

Tablature is a paint-by-number language telling you which notes to play on the fingerboard. Each of the six lines represents a string on the guitar. The numbers on the line indicate which frets to press down. Note that tablature does not indicate the rhythm.

1st string	E
2nd string	B
3rd string	G
4th string	D
5th string	A
6th string	E

NOTATION LEGEND

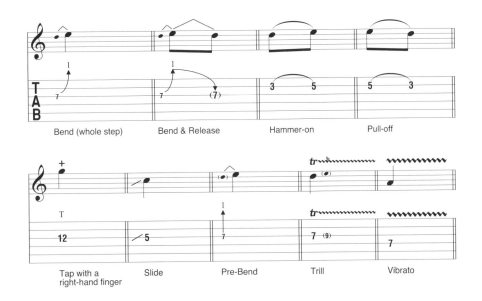

Bend (half step or whole step):

Pick the note and bend up a half step (one fret) or a whole step (two frets).

Bend & Release:

Pick the note and bend up a whole step, then release the bend back to the original note. All three notes are tied together; only the first note is attacked.

Hammer-on:

Pick the first (lower) note, then "hammer on" to sound the higher note with another finger by fretting it without picking.

Pull-off:

Place both fingers on the notes to be sounded. Pick the first (higher) note, then sound the lower note by "pulling off" the finger on the higher note while keeping the lower note fretted.

Tap:

Hammer ("tap") the fret indicated with the "pick-hand" index or middle finger and pull off to the note fretted by the fret hand.

Slide:

Strike the first note, and then, without striking it again, use the same left-hand finger to slide up or down the string to the second note.

Trill:

Very rapidly alternate between notes indicated by continuously hammering on and pulling off.

Vibrato:

Vibrate the note by rapidly bending and releasing the string using a left-hand finger, wrist, or forearm.

Finger Number:

Suggested fingerings are included under the tab staff for all examples. However, you should experiment with different fingerings and play the one that feels most comfortable to you.

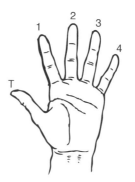

T = thumb
1 = 1st finger
2 = 2nd finger
3 = 3rd finger
4 = 4th finger

SOME MUSICAL TERMS TO KNOW

Let's review some basic music terms, which should help you understand the next sections better.

Whole-step:

The distance between any two notes that are two frets apart. For example: C to D, or F to G.

Half-step:

The distance between any two notes that are one fret apart. For example: C to C♯, or E to F.

Scale Degrees:

A method of describing tones in terms of their position in a scale. The first note or root is referred to as the "1st degree," the second note of the scale is referred to as the "2nd degree," the third note of the scale is referred to as the "3rd degree," and so on. In this book you will also see ♭3 or ♯4, which means the third note or the 3rd degree of the mode or scale is flatted or lowered a half-step down, or the 4th degree of the mode or scale is sharped or raised, as is the case of the ♯4.

WHAT IS A MODE?

A mode is a series of notes in which there is one principal note (root) to which all the others are related. In other words, the first and last note of a mode define the tonality of the mode, while it is the step-pattern or the sequence of the rest of the notes that establish its modality, its own round characteristics. For example, take C Ionian (see the following diagram). It begins and ends on C: therefore, C is its "tonality." Its step-pattern is whole step (C to D), whole-step (D to E), half-step (E to F), whole-step (F to G), whole-step (G to A), whole-step (A to B), and half-step (B to C). This step-pattern defines the Ionian Mode. Following this same step-pattern and starting and ending on, say, G, you would be playing G Ionian. You may have noticed that the Ionian Mode is the same as a major scale. So if you know how to play a major scale, you already know the Ionian Mode. As you explore each mode, you will find that we have presented its basic formula in a step-pattern and in scale degrees.

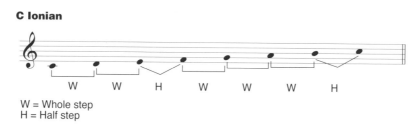

C Ionian

W = Whole step
H = Half step

The step pattern which defines the "sound" of a mode can be generated simply by taking a scale, a major scale, for example, and by altering the tonic note or the note the modes start and end on. Because there are seven notes in the scale, there are seven places to start a scale, and, therefore seven modes can be created out of the major scale. Similarly, the harmonic minor and the melodic minor scales will each produce seven modes. In this book we will only be looking at the seven modes generated by the major scale and two modes coming from the harmonic minor scale that are popular in rock music. Other modes you should explore that are not contained here include the five other modes from the harmonic minor scale and the seven modes from the melodic minor scale.

SEVEN MODES FROM THE MAJOR SCALE

This section presents the seven modes generated from the major scale. Familiarize yourself with Diagram 2. It shows you the modal relationships in the C major scale (C, D, E, F, G, A, B, C). We just saw that the Ionian Mode is the same as a major scale and that Ionian is a mode starting and ending on the first degree of the major scale. The mode starting and ending on the 2nd degree of the major scale is called Dorian. Using the diagram of the C major scale, we see that the 2nd degree of the scale is D. So, starting on the D and playing the eight notes of the C major scale D to D would be playing the D Dorian Mode (D, E, F, G, A, B, C, D). The mode starting and ending on the 3rd degree of the C major scale is called Phrygian. Can you guess which letter name the scale would be named by? The mode starting and ending on the 4th degree of the C major scale is called F Lydian. The mode starting and ending on the 5th degree of the C major scale is called G Mixolydian. The mode starting and ending on the 6th degree of the C major scale is called A Aeolian. Finally, the mode starting and ending on the 7th degree of the C major scale is called B Locrian.

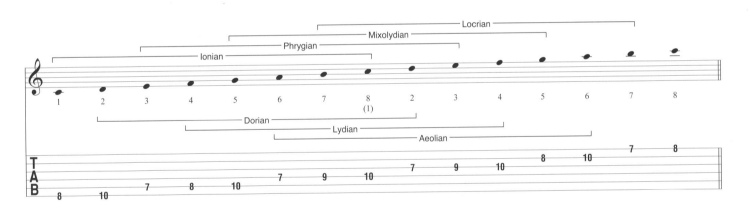

The mode names, Greek in origin, remain the same for each degree of any major scale. For example, the Phrygian Mode starts and ends on the third degree of any major scale. If you are using the C major scale (C, D, E, F, G, A, B), then it will be E Phrygian. If you are using the A major scale (A, B C♯, D, E, F♯, G♯), then it will be C♯ Phrygian. We know that Dorian starts and ends on the 2nd degree of any major scale. So A Dorian takes its name based on the G major scale (G, A, B, C, D, E, F♯), where A is the second degree in the scale. This relationship holds true for all of the modes and all of the major scales.

As mentioned earlier, there are many ways to look at a mode. The individual section on each mode will include a diagram which shows you different ways to look at each mode. In other words how a mode can be derived from different scale sources, including pentatonic scales, the major scale, and the natural minor scale. Whichever way makes sense to you is the way to approach your understanding of the modes. They are all just different ways of looking at (and playing) the same thing.

In presenting the individual modes, you will find a diagram for each one that gives you the basic formula for the mode, five basic fingering patterns throughout the neck, all of the notes of the mode on the entire fingerboard, some musical examples based on the mode, and a typical chord progression for each mode. If you play the black dots from root (R) to root (R) within each pattern, you are playing that particular mode. The white dots are also notes from the same mode in that position, and also available when you solo.

All of the fingering patterns shown for each mode in the book use C as the *tonic note* (the note the scale is based on) so that different modes can be more easily compared. To transpose it to a different key, all you need to do is move the same shape to the position where the new root is.

There are many ways to play each mode on the guitar; however, we're showing only the five basic patterns as a start. By using the diagram which shows the mode over the entire fretboard, you can discover new patterns or create your own.

We recommend that you record the chord progression on a tape recorder and then practice the mode and use it to improvise over the chords. For the musical examples, we suggest you practice each lick very slowly until you can play them very smoothly. Play a cool lick sloppily and people will hear the slop, not the lick.

> *Knowledge of theory and knowledge of music and some sort of music education is great, as long as it's fully assimilated. The problem is with people who don't assimilate it fully. It's like when you're a kid and your parents teach you how to use a knife and fork. When you're eating now you don't think about how to use a knife and fork, you are just eating. When you assimilate the technique and knowledge you don't think about it, it's just something you know how to do. It's a tool to do what you hear in your head. I think people should be afraid of ignorance.*
>
> —Reeves Gabrels (David Bowie)

THE IONIAN MODE

C Ionian

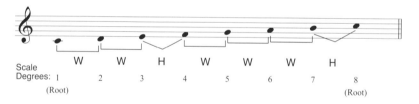

Scale Degrees:	1	2	3	4	5	6	7	8
	(Root)							(Root)

W W H W W W H

Pattern 1

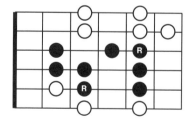

Pattern 2

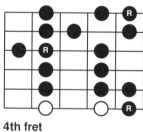

4th fret

Pattern 3

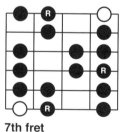

7th fret

Pattern 4

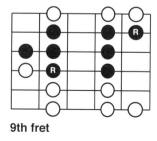

9th fret

Pattern 5

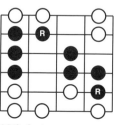

12th fret

C Ionian on the entire fretboard

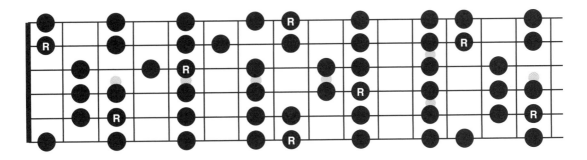

The Ionian mode is based on the 1st degree of the scale. C Ionian (C, D, E, F, G, A, B) comes from the C major scale where C is the first degree of the scale. Let's start by exploring the C Ionian Mode, beginning on the 5th fret (4th position) as shown in Pattern 2 of the Ionian fingering diagram. You'll notice this pattern contains the familiar Chuck Berry/C major pentatonic "box scale" with the addition of two notes, the 4th (F) and the 7th (B). For many rock guitarists, this will be the most familiar way to look at the Ionian Mode. Another way is to realize that this is the household-variety major scale; the familiar do, re, mi, fa, sol, la, ti, do, sound. It is commonly used over a major chord (C), a major 7th chord (Cmaj7), or a power chord (C5). E Ionian is the sound of the solos on "Blue Sky" and "Mountain Jam" by The Allman Brothers.

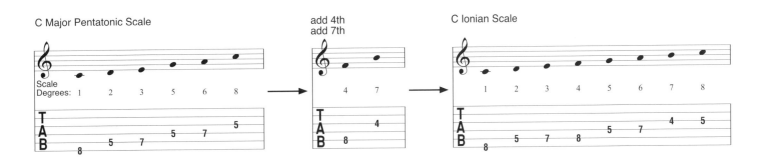

Ex. 1 is a step-wise riff from Night Ranger's "Don't Tell Me You Love Me." We have transposed this lick from A Ionian to C Ionian.

EX. 1

Ex. 2 was inspired by Dickie Betts' melody in The Allman Brothers' "Jessica." (A Ionian)

EX. 2

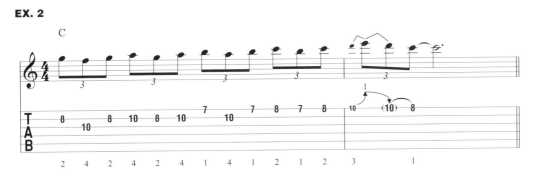

Ex. 3 is a chord progression for C Ionian.

EX. 3

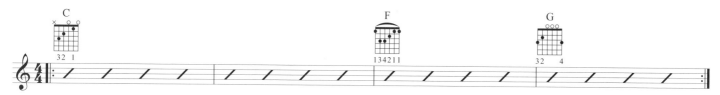

THE DORIAN MODE

C Dorian

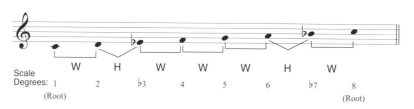

Pattern 1

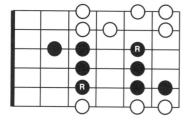

Pattern 2

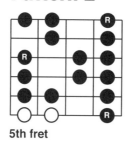

5th fret

Pattern 3

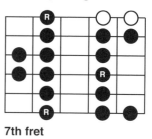

7th fret

Pattern 4

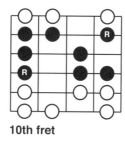

10th fret

Pattern 5

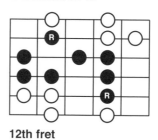

12th fret

C Dorian on the entire fretboard

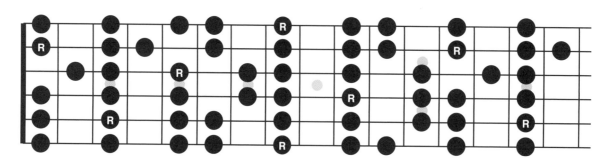

Dorian is the mode based on the 2nd degree of the major scale. C Dorian (C, D, E♭, F, G, A, B♭) comes from the B♭ major scale, where C is the 2nd degree in the scale. Start with the C Dorian Mode beginning on the 8th fret (7th position), as shown in Pattern 3 of the Dorian fingering diagram. You'll notice this pattern contains the familiar Chuck Berry/C minor pentatonic "box scale" with the addition of two notes, A and D. The sound of the Dorian Mode is quite popular and commonly used in rock music. If you've ever jammed on The Allman Brothers' "Whipping Post." you've used A Dorian. The A Dorian sound can also be heard in Santana's "Oye Come Va." A Dorian has the same characteristic sound and patterns as C Dorian, just transposed down three frets! The Dorian Mode will work over a minor chord (Cm), a minor 7th chord (Cm7), or a power chord (C5).

Different ways to look at C Dorian:
1. C Minor Pentatonic with 2nd (D) and 6th (A) added.
2. B♭ Major Scale starting from the 2nd degree, C.
3. C Major Scale with lowered 3rd (E♭) and 7th (B♭).
4. C Natural Minor with raised 6th (A).

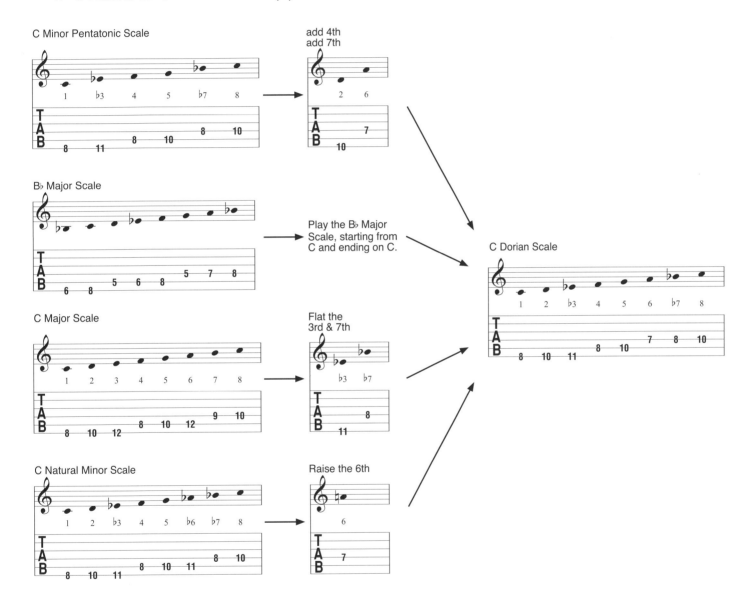

Ex. 4 reminds us of Steely Dan's "Josie." It has been transposed from F Dorian to C Dorian.

EX. 4

Ex. 5 is inspired by a line from The Allman Brothers' "Whipping Post. (A Dorian)

EX. 5

Ex. 6 is a Dorian run reflecting a Kirk Hammett line in Metallica's "For Whom the Bell Tolls." (E Dorian)

EX. 6

Ex. 7 may remind you of Joe Satriani's "Surfing with the Alien." (C Dorian)

EX. 7

Ex. 8 is a bit of tapping, inspired from a lick that Eddie Van Halen played in the song "5150." While fretting the 7th fret, 3rd string with your first finger, tap the 11th fret with your right-hand first or second finger. Then pull off the right hand and hammer on to the E note at the 9th fret with your left-hand third finger. Timing is crucial, so practice this slowly at first, and, remember you can also play the lick without tapping. (B Dorian)

EX. 8

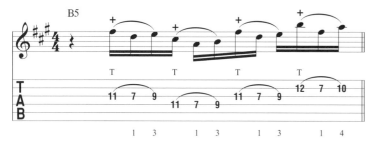

Exs. 9–10 are chord progressions for C Dorian.

EX. 9

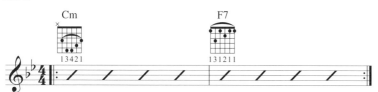

EX. 10

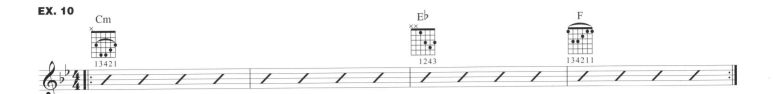

Exs. 11–12 are chord progressions for A Dorian.

EX. 11

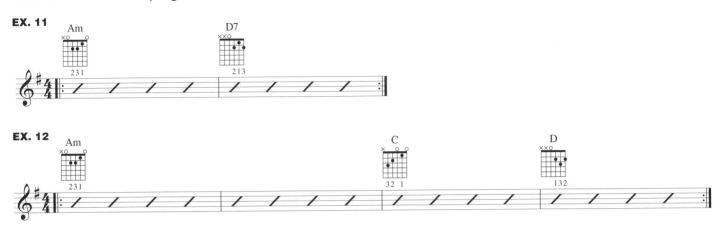

EX. 12

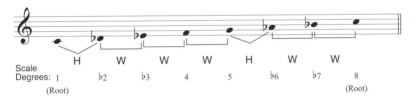

> *It's good to learn the mechanics of music, all your modes. They come in handy. They are great to have.*
>
> —*Ernie C (Body Count)*

THE PHRYGIAN MODE

C Phrygian

Pattern 1

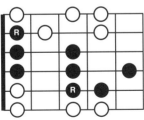

Pattern 2

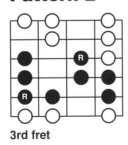

3rd fret

Pattern 3

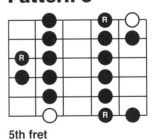

5th fret

Pattern 4

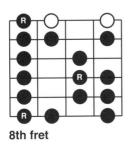

8th fret

Pattern 5

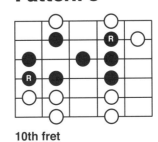

10th fret

C Phrygian on the entire fretboard

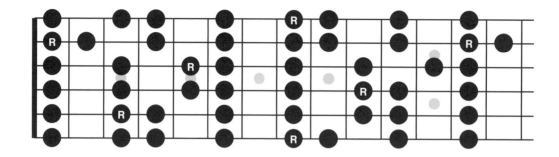

Phrygian is the mode based on the 3rd degree of the major scale. C Phrygian (C, D♭, E♭, F, G, A♭, B♭) comes from the A♭ major scale, where C is the 3rd degree of the scale. Start With the C Phrygian Mode beginning on the 8th fret as shown in Pattern 4 of the Phrygian fingering diagram. You'll notice this pattern contains the familiar Chuck Berry/C minor pentatonic "box scale" with the addition of two notes, D♭ and A♭. The Spanish sound of the Phrygian Mode is another favorite among rock guitarists, especially with Bach-rockers like Yngwie Malmsteen and Randy Rhoads and fusion players like Al DiMeola. The Phrygian Mode will work over a major chord (C), a minor chord (Cm), minor 7th chord (Cm7) or a power chord (C5).

Different ways to look at C Phrygian:
1. C Minor Pentatonic with ♭2nd (D♭) and ♭6th (A♭) added.
2. A♭ Major Scale starting from the 3rd degree, C.
3. C Major Scale with lowered 2nd (D♭), 3rd (E♭), 6th (A♭), and 7th (B♭).
4. C Natural Minor with lowered 2nd (D♭).

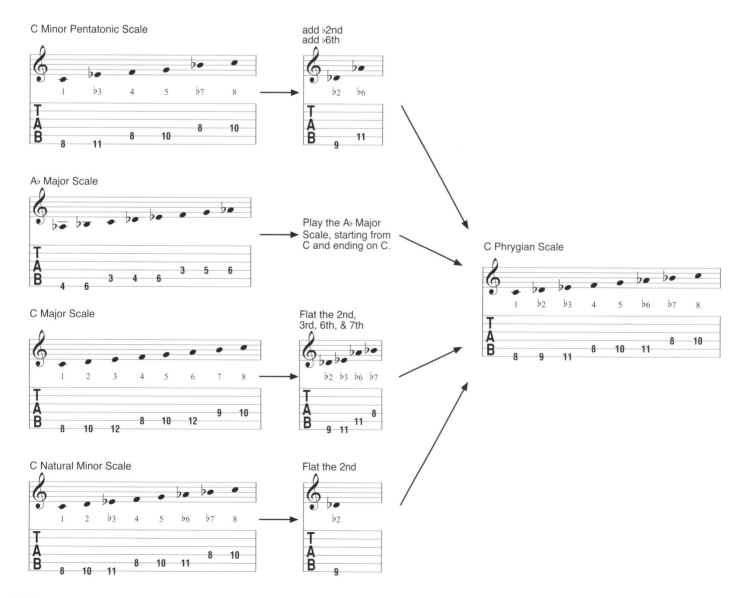

Ex. 13 is based on "Malaguena." It has been transposed from A Phrygian to C Phrygian.

EX. 13

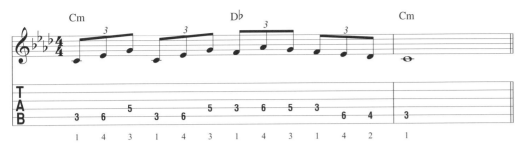

Ex. 14 was inspired by King Diamond's "Abigail." (E Phrygian)

EX. 14

Ex. 15. The Phrygian Mode is not just used by the classical-metal crowd. This example is reminiscent of "I Remember California" by R.E.M. (E Phrygian)

EX. 15

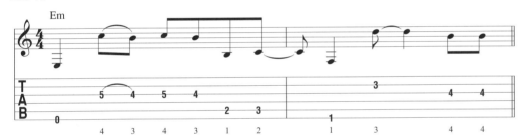

Ex. 16 resembles an Alex Lifeson line from Rush's "La Villa Strangiato." (E Phrygian)

EX. 16

Exs. 17–18 are chord progressions for C Phrygian.

EX. 17

EX. 18

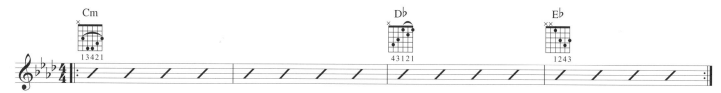

Exs. 19–20 are chord progressions for E Phrygian.

EX. 19

EX. 20

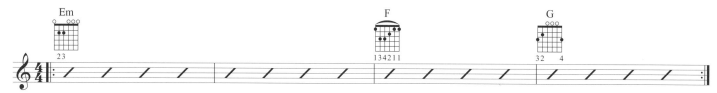

> Traditional theory is basically a historical perspective of tonal music. It doesn't mean you have to always do it that way. 99% of the songs you hear people play are centered on tonal music. Somebody who knows the modes and knows how to analyze music is at an advantage in any situation that we would call music, regardless of the style.
>
> —Steve Morse

THE LYDIAN MODE

C Lydian

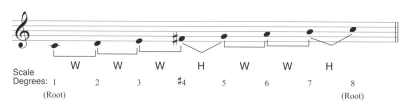

Scale Degrees:	1 (Root)	2	3	♯4	5	6	7	8 (Root)
	W	W	W	H	W	W	H	

Pattern 1

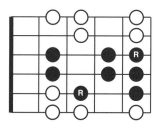

Pattern 2

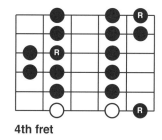

4th fret

Pattern 3

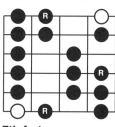

7th fret

Pattern 4

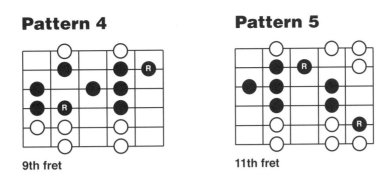

9th fret

Pattern 5

11th fret

C Lydian on the entire fretboard

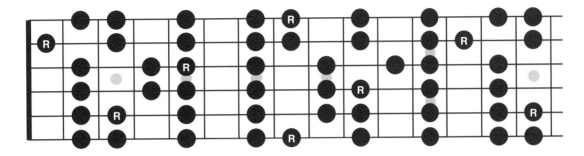

Lydian is the mode based on the 4th degree of the major scale. C Lydian (C, D, E, F♯, G, A, B) takes its name from the G major scale, where C is the 4th degree of the scale. Let's start with the C Lydian Mode beginning on the 4th fret (5th position) as shown in Pattern 2 of the Lydian fingering diagram. You'll notice this pattern contains the familiar Chuck Berry/C major pentatonic "box scale" with the addition of two notes, the ♯4 (F♯) and the 7th (B). Some consider this a slightly "outside" sound. While it is not widely used in rock music, it is a favorite of guitarists like Steve Vai and Joe Satriani. The Lydian mode will work over a major chord (C), a major 7th chord (Cmaj7), a major 7♯11 (Cmaj7♯11), or a power chord (C5).

Different ways to look at C Lydian:
1. C Major Pentatonic with ♯4th (F♯) and 7th (B) added.
2. G Major Scale starting from the 4th degree (C).
3. C Major Scale with raised 4th (F♯).

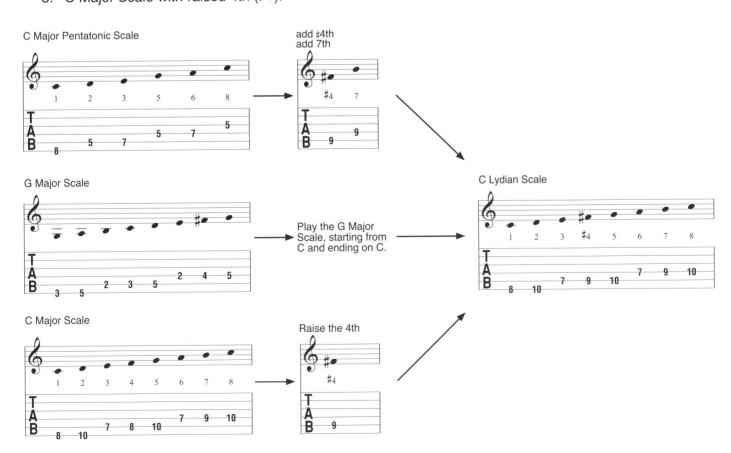

Ex. 21 is based on a melody from Joe Satriani. (C Lydian)

EX. 21

Ex. 22 is similar to a line from Poison's "Talk Dirty to Me." (G Lydian)

EX. 22

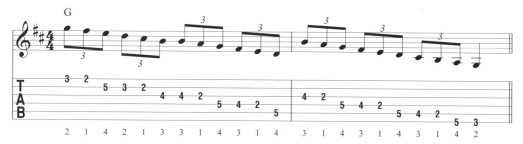

Ex. 23 reminds us of a line from Rush's "Free Will." (F Lydian)

EX. 23

Ex. 24 was inspired by an Al Pitrelli melody using hammer-ons, pull-offs, and a bit of tapping. (D Lydian)

EX. 24

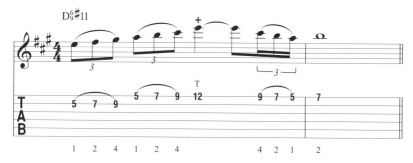

Ex. 25 is a take on Steve Vai's "Call It Sleep." (B♭ Lydian)

EX. 25

Ex. 26 is a reflection of something we heard Jake E. Lee do on Ozzy Osbourne's "Lightning Strikes." (C Lydian)

EX. 26

Ex. 27 is a Randy Rhoads/"Mr. Crowley"-inspired lick, which features hammer-ons and pull-offs using three-notes per-string. (B♭ Lydian)

EX. 27

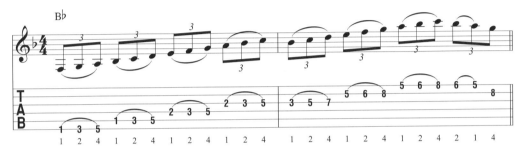

Exs. 28–29 are chord progressions for C Lydian.

EX. 28

EX. 29

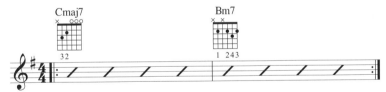

Ex. 30 is a chord progression for F Lydian.

EX. 30

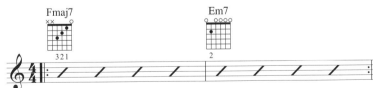

> If you know the major scale, you know all the modes, as they are all derived from the scale. Memorize the sound of the modes; it's not just a finger process, it's a whole thing with moods. If you can memorize that mood, you can call upon it when you want to. My favorite mode is Lydian. I always think of it in an Egyptian setting; it sounds mystical. It's a subtle mode when used in a subtle context. In the Baroque period, Lydian used to be reminiscent of devil music, because it had the sharp four that was supposed to invoke the devil. That's ridiculous.
>
> —Steve Vai

THE MIXOLYDIAN MODE

C Mixolydian

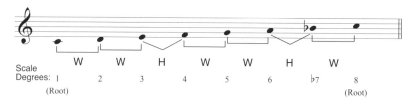

Scale Degrees: 1 (Root) — W — 2 — W — 3 — H — 4 — W — 5 — W — 6 — H — ♭7 — W — 8 (Root)

Pattern 1

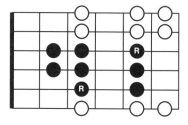

Pattern 2

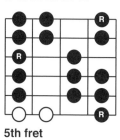

5th fret

Pattern 3

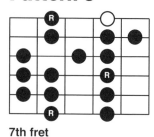

7th fret

Pattern 4

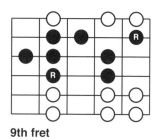

9th fret

Pattern 5

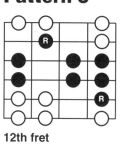

12th fret

C Mixolydian on the entire fretboard

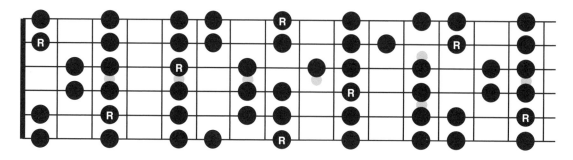

Mixolydian is the mode based on the 5th degree of the major scale. C Mixolydian (C, D, E, F, G, A, B♭) takes its name from the F major scale, where C is the 5th degree of the scale. Let's start with the C Mixolydian Mode beginning on the 5th fret, as shown in Pattern 2 of the Mixolydian fingering diagram. You'll notice this pattern contains the familiar Chuck Berry/C major pentatonic "box scale" with the addition of two notes, the 4th (F) and the ♭7th (B♭). The Mixolydian Mode is often favored by rock guitarists. It works over a major chord C, a dominant 7th chord (C7), and a power chord (C5).

Because the flatted 7th turns any major chord (C) into a dominant 7th (C7), the Mixolydian mode is the most commonly played dominant chord scale. In other words, the C Mixolydian Mode is a natural for playing over the C7 chord. It's the same for A Mixolydian and A7, and so on.

Different ways to look at C Mixolydian:
1. C Major Pentatonic with 4th (F) and ♭7th (B♭) added.
2. F Major Scale starting from the 5th degree (C).
3. C Major Scale with flatted 7th (B♭).

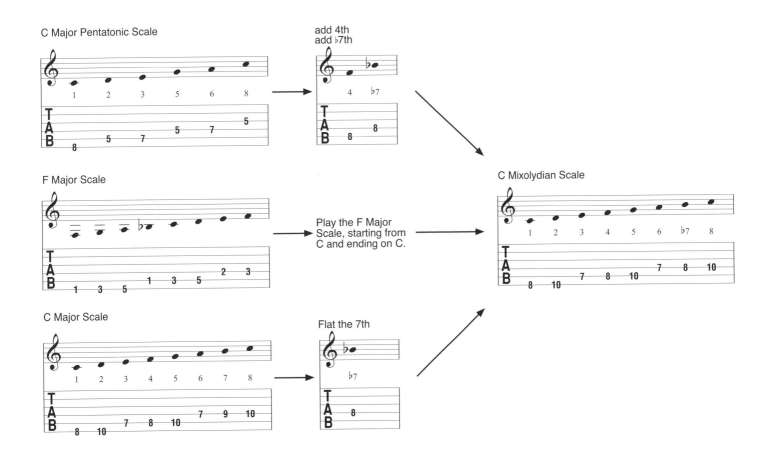

Ex. 31 is based on a Randy Rhoads line from Ozzy Osbourne's "Mr. Crowley." (C Mixolydian)

EX. 31

Ex. 32 reminds us of a line from "Freeway Jam," by Jeff Beck. (C Mixolydian)

EX. 32

Ex. 33 is a taste of Mixo inspired by Ratt's "You're In Love." (D Mixolydian)

EX. 33

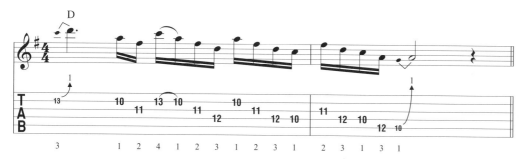

Ex. 34 is based on a Jerry Garcia line from The Grateful Dead's "China Cat Sunflower." (G Mixolydian)

EX. 34

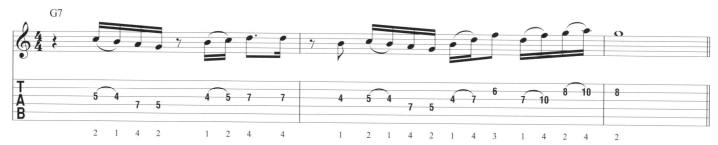

Ex. 35 reminds us of a line in Aerosmith's "Walk This Way." (C Mixolydian)

EX. 35

Ex. 36 has its roots in "Paradise City" from Guns N' Roses. (C Mixolydian)

EX. 36

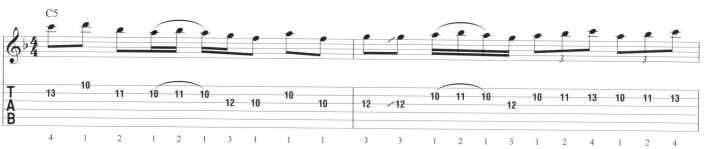

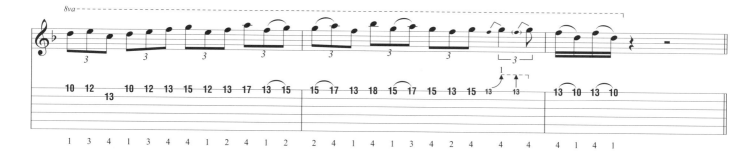

Exs. 37–38 are chord progressions for C Mixolydian.

EX. 37

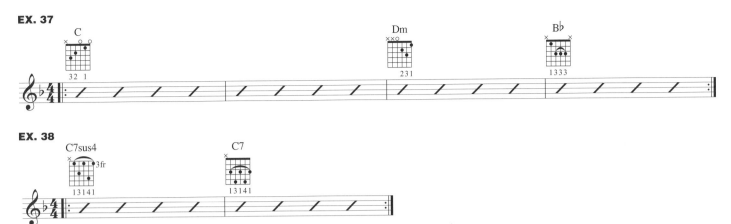

EX. 38

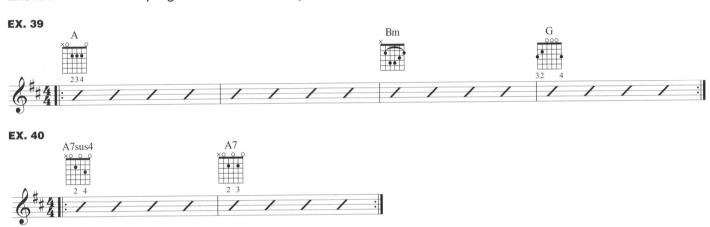

Exs. 39–40 are chord progressions for A Mixolydian.

EX. 39

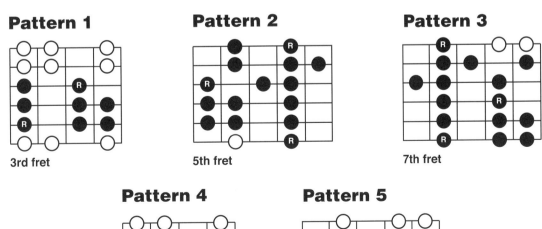

EX. 40

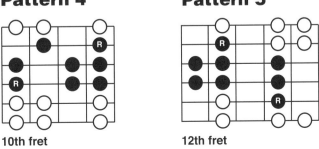

THE AEOLIAN MODE

C Aeolian

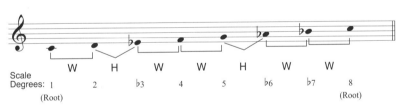

Scale Degrees: 1 (Root) 2 ♭3 4 5 ♭6 ♭7 8 (Root)
W H W W H W W

Pattern 1
3rd fret

Pattern 2
5th fret

Pattern 3
7th fret

Pattern 4
10th fret

Pattern 5
12th fret

C Aeolian on the entire fretboard

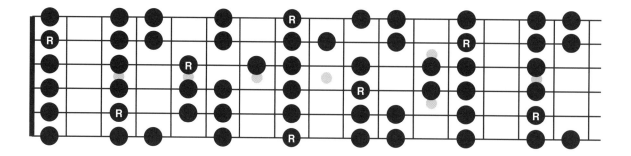

Aeolian is the mode based on the 6th degree of the scale. C Aeolian (C, D, E♭, F, G, A♭, B♭) takes its name from the E♭ major scale, where C is the 6th note in the scale. Let's start with the C Aeolian Mode beginning on the 7th fret, as shown in Pattern 3 of the Aeolian fingering diagram. You'll notice this pattern contains the familiar Chuck Berry/C minor pentatonic "box scale" with the addition of two notes, the 2nd (D) and the ♭6th (A♭). Another name for the Aeolian Mode is the natural minor scale. Aeolian is the most commonly used mode in rock and heavy metal and a favorite of bands ranging from Ozzy to Soul Asylum. The Aeolian Mode works over a minor chord (Cm), a minor 7th chord (Cm7), or a power chord (C5).

Different ways to look at C Aeolian:
1. C Minor Pentatonic with 2nd (D) and ♭6th (A♭) added.
2. E♭ Major Scale starting from the 6th degree, C.
3. C Major Scale with lowered 3rd (E♭), 6th (A♭), and 7th (B♭).
4. C Dorian with lowered 6th (A♭).

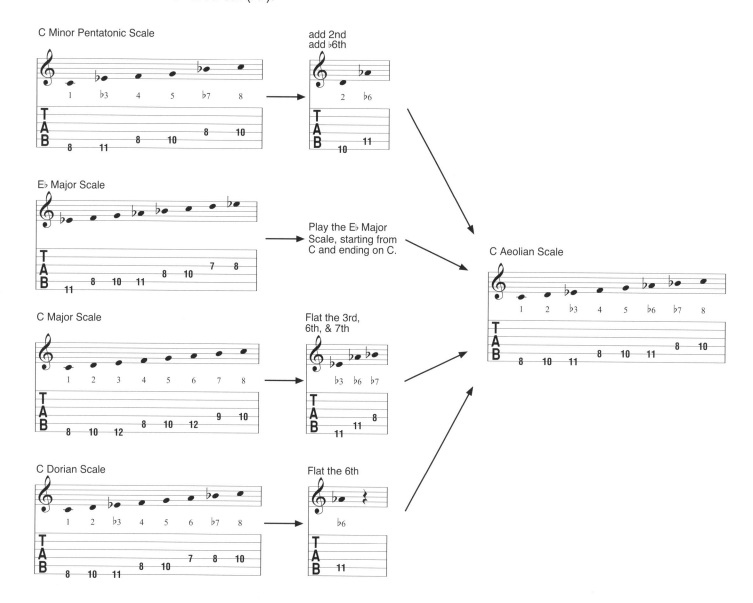

Ex. 41 has its roots in a Randy Rhoads line from Ozzy Osbourne's "Over the Mountain." (C Aeolian)

EX. 41

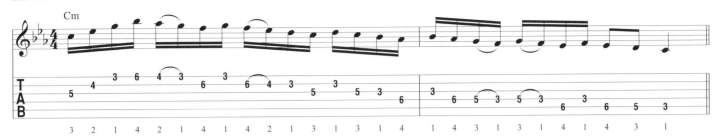

Ex. 42 comes from "Wasted Years" by Iron Maiden. It's a good example of what you can do with just one string. (E Aeolian)

EX. 42

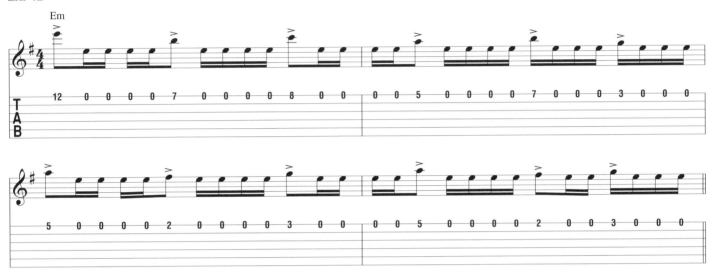

Ex. 43 is our take on Vito Bratta's solo for White Lion's "Wait." (A Aeolian)

EX. 43

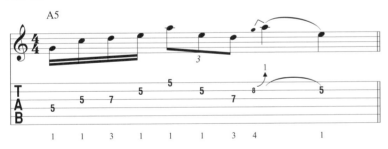

Ex. 44 is a take on another line Randy played in Ozzy's "You Can't Kill Rock 'n' Roll." (F♯ Aeolian)

EX. 44

Ex. 45 was inspired by Vinnie Moore's "Daydream." (G Aeolian)

EX. 45

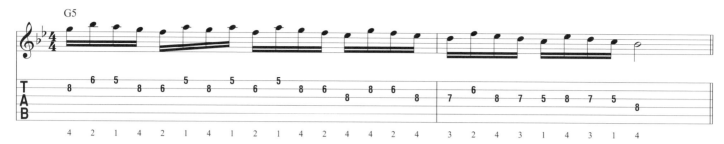

Ex. 46 echoes Steve Howe from Yes' "Heart of the Sunrise." (A Aeolian)

EX. 46

Ex. 47 is our take of a Vivian Campbell line from Dio's "Rainbow in the Dark." (A Aeolian)

EX. 47

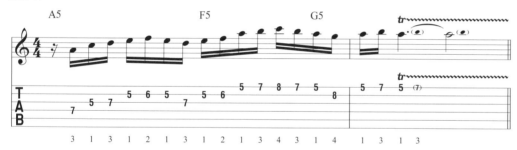

Ex. 48 is an Yngwie Malmsteen-like line from "Hiroshima Mon Amour." (B Aeolian)

EX. 48

Exs. 49–50 are chord progressions for C Aeolian.

EX. 49

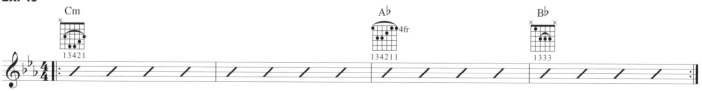

EX. 50

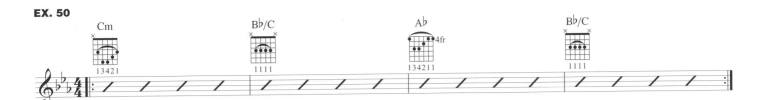

Exs. 51–52 are chord progressions for A Aeolian.

EX. 51

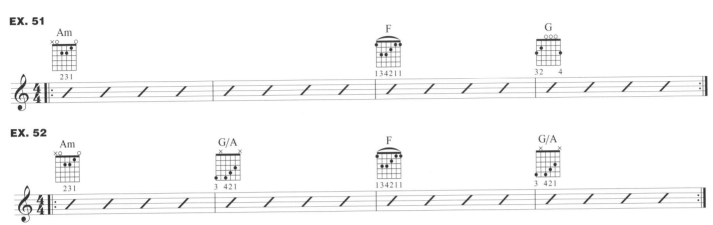

EX. 52

Instead of learning constantly from the same source, I say try to have the widest variety of input. Kids will listen to certain guitarists. I say listen to as many different things as you can, even if you don't know who they are or what they are doing, just have that input. Eventually, it's going to come out in some form or another. Combine that with scales and different flexibilities so you can put off what you want.

—George Lynch (Dokken)

THE LOCRIAN MODE

C Locrian

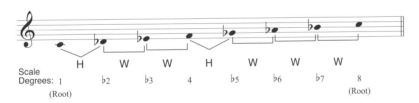

Pattern 1

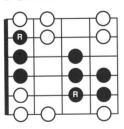

Pattern 2

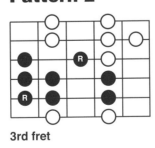

3rd fret

Pattern 3

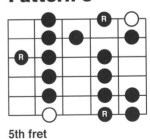

5th fret

Pattern 4

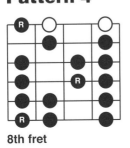

8th fret

Pattern 5

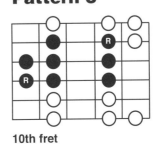

10th fret

C Locrian on the entire fretboard

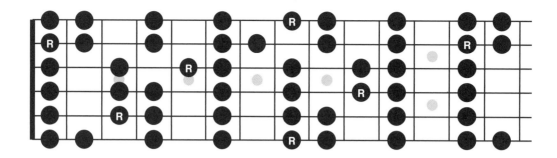

Locrian is the mode based on the 7th degree of the major scale. C Locrian (C, D♭, E♭, F, G♭, A♭, B♭) takes its name from the D♭ major scale where C is the 7th note in the scale. Let's start with the C Locrian Mode beginning on the 6th fret, as shown in Pattern 3 of the Locrian fingering diagram. You'll notice this pattern contains the familiar Chuck Berry/D♭ major pentatonic "box scale" with the addition of two notes, the 4th (G♭) and the 7th (C). The Locrian Mode is rarely used in rock music, but primarily shows up in jazz. The Locrian Mode works over a minor 7♭5 chord (Cm7♭5) or a diminished triad (C°).

Different ways to look at C Locrian:
1. D♭ Major Pentatonic with 4th (G♭) and 7th (C) added.
2. D♭ Major Scale starting from the 7th degree, C.
3. C Major Scale with lowered 2nd (D♭), 3rd (E♭), 5th (G♭), and 7th (B♭).
4. C Natural Minor with flatted 2nd (D♭), and 5th (G♭).

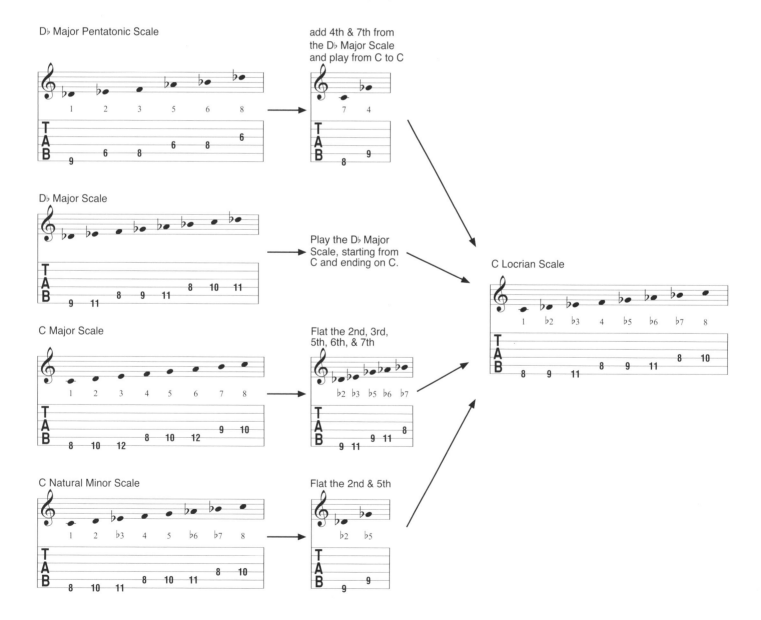

Ex. 53 is reminiscent of a Randy Rhoads line from Ozzy Osbourne's "Mr. Crowley." It has been transposed from E Locrian to C Locrian.

EX. 53

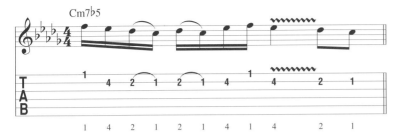

Ex. 54 was inspired by the intro to Metallica's "Seek and Destroy." (A Locrian)

EX. 54

TWO MODES FROM THE HARMONIC MINOR SCALE

This section presents two modes generated from the harmonic minor scale: C Harmonic Minor Scale and C Spanish-Gypsy Scale (5th mode of the harmonic minor scale). Again, all patterns use C as the tonic note, but you should explore these ideas and sounds in other keys as well.

THE HARMONIC MINOR SCALE

C Harmonic Minor

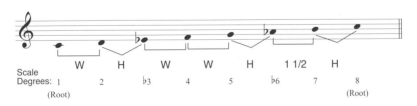

Pattern 1

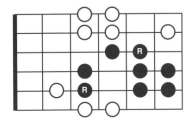

Pattern 2

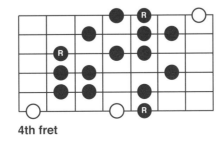

4th fret

Pattern 3

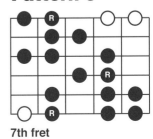

7th fret

Pattern 4   Pattern 5

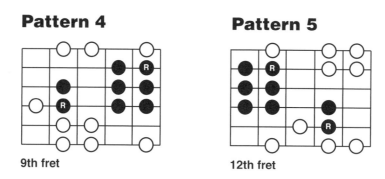

9th fret   12th fret

C Harmonic Minor on the entire fretboard

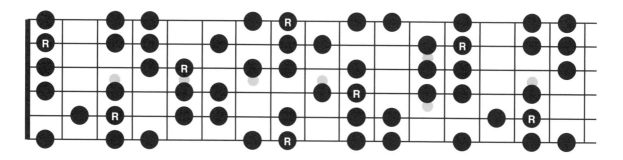

The harmonic minor scale has an exotic—and some would say evil—sound favored by many rock players. Certainly Randy Rhoads and Yngwie Malmsteen come to mind. It is used over a minor chord (Cm), a minor-major 7th chord (Cm(maj7)), or a power chord (C5).

Different ways to look at the C Harmonic Minor Scale:
1. C Natural Minor Scale (or C Aeolian) with raised 7th (B).
2. C Major Scale with flatted 3rd (E♭) and 6th (A♭).
3. C Phrygian Scale with raised 2nd (D) and 7th (B).

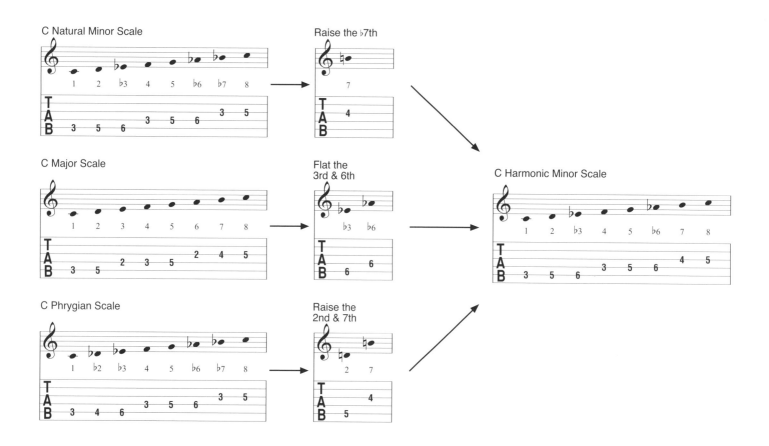

Ex. 55 is an altered bit from Vinnie Moore's "Daydream." It has been transposed from D Harmonic Minor to C Harmonic Minor.

EX. 55

Ex. 56 is a take on Tony MacAlpine's "Quarter to Midnight." (E Harmonic Minor)

EX. 56

Ex. 57 is another line inspired by Vinnie Moore's "Daydream." (D Harmonic Minor)

EX. 57

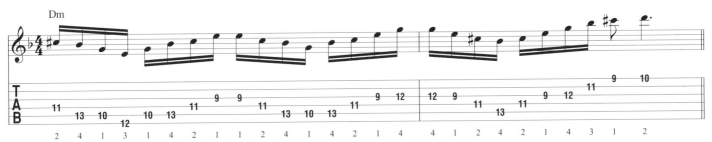

Ex. 58 is a chord progression for A Harmonic Minor.

EX. 58

Ex. 59 is a chord progression for C Harmonic Minor.

EX. 59

THE SPANISH-GYPSY SCALE:
5TH MODE OF THE HARMONIC MINOR SCALE

C Spanish-Gypsy

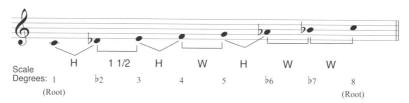

Pattern 1

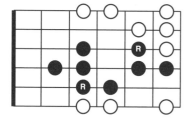

Pattern 2

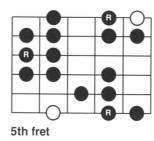

5th fret

Pattern 3

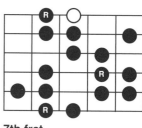

7th fret

Pattern 4

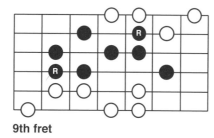

9th fret

Pattern 5

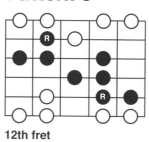

12th fret

C Spanish-Gypsy on the entire fretboard

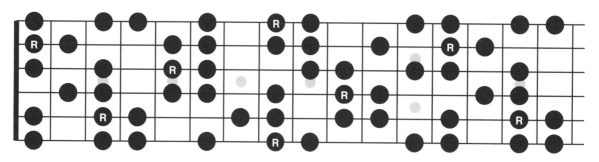

The sound of this mode is very popular in rock, metal and jazz. It's mainly used over a major chord (C), a dominant chord (C7), or a power chord (C5).

Different ways to look at the C Spanish-Gypsy Scale:
1. F Harmonic Minor Scale starting from 5th degree (C).
2. C Phrygian Scale with raised 3rd (E).
3. C Mixolydian Scale with flatted 2nd (D♭) and 6th (A♭).

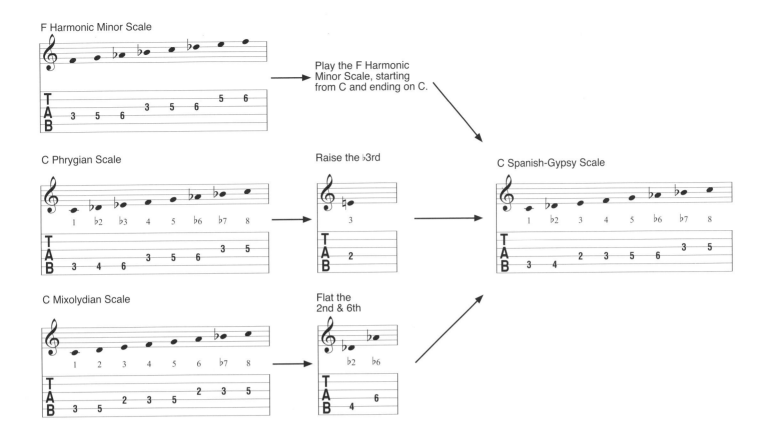

Play the F Harmonic Minor Scale, starting from C and ending on C.

Ex. 60 is a take from Yngwie Malmsteen's "I'll See the Light Tonight." It has been transposed from E Spanish-Gypsy or A Harmonic Minor to C Spanish-Gypsy or F Harmonic Minor.

EX. 60

Ex. 61 is a bit inspired from "Master of Puppets" by Metallica. (B Spanish-Gypsy or E Harmonic Minor over B7)

EX. 61

Ex. 62 is an Ulrich Roth-type line. (B Spanish-Gypsy or E Harmonic Minor over B)

EX. 62

Exs. 63–64 are chord progressions for C Spanish-Gypsy (F Harmonic Minor).

EX. 63

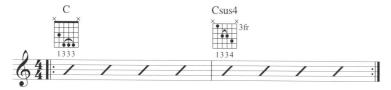

EX. 64

Exs. 65–66 are chord progressions for E Spanish-Gypsy (A Harmonic Minor).

EX. 65

EX. 66

MOVING FROM ONE MODE TO ANOTHER

When playing over a chord progression, one of the most effective ways to change your sound is to change your mode. Even when playing over one chord that doesn't change, you can still change your sound and make the music more interesting by changing your mode.

We'll give you some musical examples that demonstrate moving modes and a chord progression for you to record and use to practice shifting from one mode to another. Don't forget to try this in different keys as well.

Ex. 67 is a take on how Randy Rhoads used modes on Ozzy Osbourne's "Mr. Crowley."

EX. 67

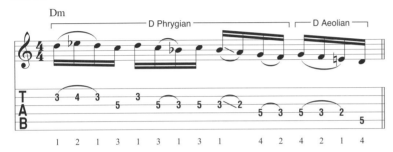

Ex. 68 shows you how different modes can be used in Motley Crue's "Girls Girls Girls."

EX. 68

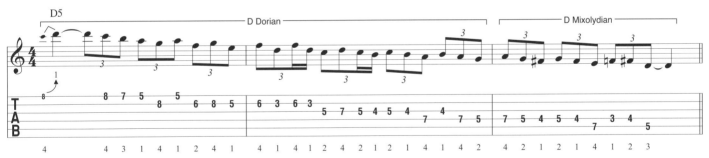

Ex. 69 was inspired by Jake E. Lee navigating the changes in Ozzy's "Bark at the Moon."

EX. 69

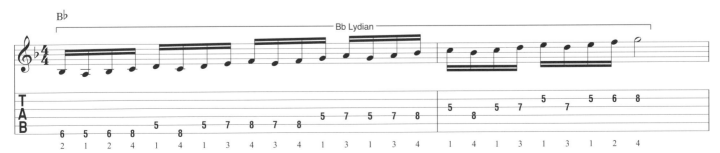

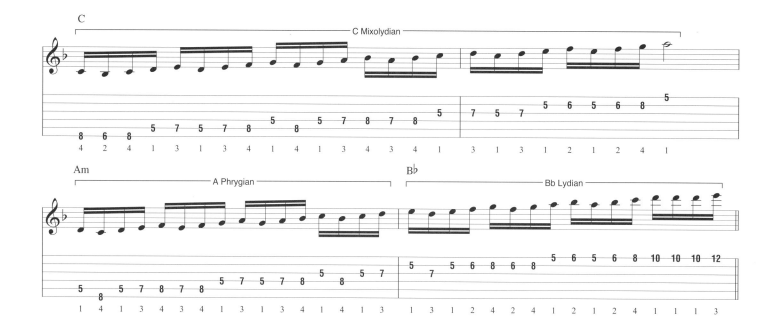

Ex. 70 is a chord progression to practice shifting between modes.

EX. 70

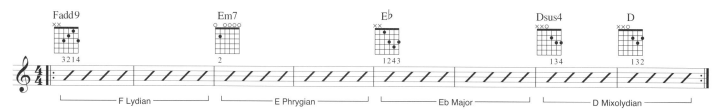

I started to make myself aware of what note choices blues players used. It's an art of combining Dorian, Mixolydian, and the Blues Scale and using all of those notes to where it sounds hip. If you combine Dorian and Mixolydian, which are both seven-note scales, you get an eight-note scale before it repeats with the octave. For the Mr. Big song "Wind Me Up," the solo is B Dorian and Mixolydian. I use my eight-note scale. Start with the 14th position low E string, on the F# note. The shape would be a whole step and a half step for the lowest two strings. F#, G#, A, B, C#, D. The next two strings would be 11th position with a half step and a whole step shape using E#, E, F#, G#, A, and B. On the B string you shift back to the 14th position and do three half steps, C#, D, D#. Then I skip the fourth E, which isn't that strong a chord tone, and go to the 5th, F#, which makes it easier to play because you get to stay in the 14th position. It's cool because you can keep it three notes per string and end up getting a 7th. The high E string is F#, G#, and A. I'd much rather have those three notes than starting on the fourth.

—Paul Gilbert (Mr. Big)

It's always been my theory that you play how you play because that's the way you always wanted to play. Then, years down the road, you start second guessing yourself. I think sometimes maybe I should have studied and played more jazz, just because I listen to it so often and I learn from it so much. But I remind myself these things (blues/rock) were what were important to me at the time. That's why I play the way I play. I can't start to second-guess myself now. I can just start relearning and trying to open new doors for my own self to learn things that maybe I wasn't capable of learning before.

—Warren Haynes (The Allman Brothers Band)

WHAT YOU CAN DO WITH THE MODES

One of the advantages of learning modes is that they provide a great way to add color and spice to your solos: you can make them bright, mysterious, or whatever. They will allow you to explore those places you've never been before by introducing you to notes that you might not have previously thought of playing.

Also, understanding how to use modes will greatly help you play over chord changes, especially busy ones. By moving from one mode to another, your solo will not only clearly define the changes you are playing over, but it will add another set of colors to those you already possess.

How you use the modes and the information contained in this book depends on you, the player. Although the harmonic function of the chord in a tune and its type, say, major or minor, often dictate what mode to use, the choice of what to play is yours. It depends on the moods and sounds you want to create and how you hear and perceive each mode.

A good way to use this book is to take your time and think of each mode as a separate guitar lesson. For example, spend a week exploring the sound of Dorian before going on to Phrygian. The more time you spend with a mode, the more comfortable you will be using it in your playing. Remember, this is not a race to memorize things, but rather an opportunity to expand your palette and expand your vocabulary for your solos.

RECOMMENDED LISTENING

Ionian Mode

"Blue Sky" — The Allman Brothers Band
"Don't Stop Believin'" — Journey
"Layla" — Derek and the Dominos

Dorian Mode

"Blue Wind" — Jeff Beck
"Girls Girls Girls" — Motley Crüe
"Sad But True" — Metallica
"Suicide Solution" — Ozzy Osbourne
"Sweating Bullets" — Megadeth
"The Extremist" — Joe Satriani

Phrygian Mode

"Dead Skin Mask" — Slayer
"I'll See the Light Tonight" — Yngwie Malmsteen
"Mediterranean Sundance" — Al DiMeola
"Mr. Scary" — Dokken
"Once" — Pearl Jam
"Skeletons in the Closet" — Anthrax
"Stardog Champion" — Mother Love Bone
"The Ancient" — Steve Howe

Lydian Mode

"Midnight Express" — Extreme
"Point of No Return" — Kansas
"Talk Dirty To Me" — Poison
"Vaseline" — Stone Temple Pilots
"You're In Love" — Ratt

Mixolydian Mode

"All Good People" — Yes
"Captain Nemo" — Michael Schenker
"China Cat Sunflower" — Grateful Dead
"Forever" — Kiss
"Hands All Over" — Soundgarden
"Jessica" — The Allman Brothers Band
"Keep Your Hands To Yourself" — The Georgia Satellites
"Kitten's Got Claws" — Whitesnake
"Lightning Strikes" — Ozzy Osbourne
"Patience" — Guns 'N' Roses
"Pepper Shake" — Greg Howe
"Strawberry Fields Forever" — The Beatles
"Sweet Emotion" — Aerosmith
"Two Rolling Stones" — Robin Trower
"Wait" — White Lion
"Who Made Who" — AC/DC
"You Know What I Mean" — Jeff Beck
"Zap" — Eric Johnson

Aeolian Mode

"Always With Me, Always With You" — Joe Satriani
"Black Star" — Yngwie Malmsteen
"Crazy Train" — Ozzy Osbourne
"Crying In the Rain" — Whitesnake
"18 and Life" — Skid Row
"Heaven Tonight" — Yngwie Malmsteen
"Hey You" — Pink Floyd
"House of Pain" — Faster Pussycat
"Kiss of Death" — Dokken
"Locked In" — Judas Priest
"Master of Puppets" — Metallica
"New Year's Day" — U2
"One" — Metallica
"Peace of Mind" — Boston
"Queen of the Reich" — Queensryche
"Rainbow in the Dark" — Dio
"Road Games" — Allan Holdsworth
"S.A.T.O." — Ozzy Osbourne
"Skyscraper" — David Lee Roth
"Somebody to Shove" — Soul Asylum
"Sweet Child 0' Mine" — Guns 'N' Roses
"The Forgotten" — Joe Satriani
"Wasted Years" — Iron Maiden
"You Give Love a Bad Name" — Bon Jovi

Locrian Mode

"Serenity in Murder" — Slayer
"Wake Up Dead" — Megadeth

INTRODUCTION

Mariah Carey and Black Sabbath are both looking to do the same thing with their music. Each of them hope to present songs that stay with you for the long haul. They are both trying to hook you. In pop music, the hook is found in the melody. In all forms of rock, be it metal, alternative, hard rock, blues rock, the hook is found in the riff. Where Boyz II Men ask you to sing along, Led Zeppelin invite you to pick up the air guitar. How many people know all the words to Deep Purple's "Smoke on the Water?" How many more people know the riff "Dun dun dun, dun dun dun-dun, dun dun dun, dun-dun?" Cool riffs and classic melodies are not mutually exclusive. The greatest bands, like The Beatles, have it both ways, with songs like "Day Tripper" and "Birthday."

Rock Riffs For Guitar is designed to show you how some of the finest guitarists used simple lines to create memorable song hooks. Mostly, the authors hope this book will be inspirational in getting you to write your own timeless riffs, perhaps by altering some of the lines you learn here. To get the pro's opinion, we went to guitarists from Pantera's Diamond Darrell to Collective Soul's Ed Roland, and asked them for the riffs that changed their lives.

We've presented here 114 rifts divided into five sections: Single-Note Riffs, Combining Single-Notes With Chords, Power-Chord Riffs, Chord-Strumming Riffs, and Arpeggio Riffs. Just spend as much time as you need with the tablature explanation, and then riff out to your heart's content.

EXPLAINING TABLATURE

Tablature is a paint-by-number language telling you which notes to play on the fingerboard. Each of the six lines represents a string on the guitar. The numbers on the line indicate which frets to press down. Note that tablature does not indicate the rhythm.

NOTATION LEGEND

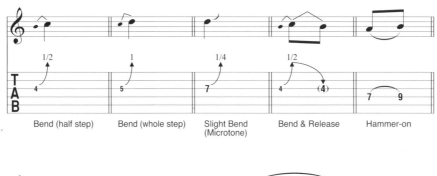

Bend (half step)   Bend (whole step)   Slight Bend (Microtone)   Bend & Release   Hammer-on

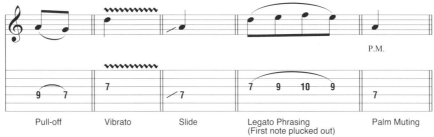

Pull-off   Vibrato   Slide   Legato Phrasing (First note plucked out)   Palm Muting

Bend (whole step):

Pick the note and bend up a whole step (two frets).

Slight Bend (microtone):

Pick the note and bend up slightly. A microtone is less than a half step (one fret).

Bend & Release:

Pick the note and bend up a whole step, then release the bend back to the original note. All three notes are tied together; only the first note is attacked.

Hammer-on:

Pick the first (lower) note, then "hammer on" to sound the higher note with another finger by fretting it without picking.

Pull-off:

Place both fingers on the notes to be sounded. Pick the first (higher) note, then sound the lower note by "pulling off" the finger on the higher note while keeping the lower note fretted.

Slide:

Strike the first note, and then, without striking it again, use the same left-hand finger to slide up or down the string to the second note.

Legato Phrasing:

A series of notes where only the first note is picked and the rest are played with hammer-ons and pull-offs.

Palm Muting:

A note or notes are played with the picking hand resting on the strings, muting the ring of each note, and adding a percussive sound in its place.

Usually a good song is a very simple thing, and you've got to open yourself up to that. Sometimes the simplest things are the coolest. I always think in terms of a hook, something to latch onto. You try and use that as a building block. I usually start with a riff, or a hook, or a chord change, and mold it so it goes somewhere.

Sometimes I'll sit down with Steven (Tyler) and we'll draw on a certain song. I'll say, "Wouldn't it be neat to write a song like something that really knocked us out when we were 15?" We went to see Keith Richards, and he played "Connection" in the show. We were thinking about how cool that song was and how cool The Kinks and that kind of English pop-rock was. I started playing a riff like that, and Steven's at the keyboard. By the end of the afternoon we had "My Girl" I think it's a tip of the hat to those songs from the '60s.

You discover riffs all different ways. If you do anything one way, it gets stale very fast. The riff to "Walk This Way" was written at a soundcheck in Hawaii. Sometimes I won't touch a guitar for days, and when I pick it up is when I get some of the best things. That's because you're not into your scales or whatever you've been practicing. The riff to "F.I.N.E" came out in as long as it took to play it. Sometimes you can have a terrible day and that's what does it. Sometimes you've got to have an attitude. But you can't actually be angry. I used to think that's what it was. It would be really good to let the dog bite you and you'd come out with some good stuff. Anger is good, but you end up realizing you play good in spite of anger. It's more like attitude and getting out some aggression. Speed metal doesn't do anything for me. I like the real power rock stuff like Deep Purple and Metallica. I still get goose bumps when I hear "Immigrant Song." "Love in an Elevator" was an interesting riff that needed a song around it. For "Don't Get Mad Get Even" I put on "Rag Doll" backwards and tried to play along with it. I got a chord change and built it from there.

—Joe Perry (Aerosmith)

SINGLE-NOTE RIFFS

You will probably recognize many of the following riffs. They are all made up of single-note lines. The Blues Scale and the Minor Pentatonic Scale are the most common sources for rock and blues guitar riffs and solos. Artists from Nirvana to Pink Floyd dip into the same pool of notes to write their riffs.

For a short review of these scales, refer to the chapters on Major and Minor Pentatonic Scales, and Basic Blues.

Ex. 1 is reminiscent of Led Zeppelin's "Heartbreaker." Notice that the riff opens with the first five notes of the A Blues Scale (A,C, D, D♯, E, G), played in order! In the hands of a composer like Jimmy Page, even a consecutive scale pattern can become a classic.

EX. 1

Ex. 2 was inspired by Jack Bruce's line from Cream's "Sunshine of Your Love." Notice that they have used all the notes of the D Blues Scale (D,F,G,A♭,A,C). Cream bassist Jack Bruce said the riff was composed on an upright bass one early dawn.

EX. 2

Ex. 3 is an Aerosmith-like line from "Walk This Way." The notes are from the E Blues Scale (E,G,A,B♭,B,D).

EX. 3

Ex. 4 is similar to the "Aqualung" riff from Jethro Tull. Just like "Heartbreaker," this riff uses the first five notes of the six-note blues scale, here played in G (G,B♭,C,D♭,D,F).

EX. 4

Ex. 5 is a Nirvana-like line inspired by "Come As You Are." It too uses five out of six notes in the blues scale, this time leaving out the D of the B Blues Scale (B,D,E,F,F♯,A).

EX. 5

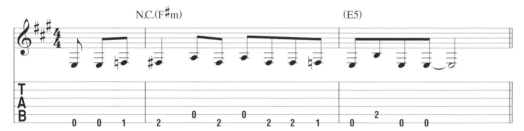

Ex. 6 reminds us of a line from "I Want to Take You Higher" by Sly and the Family Stone. This descending line uses the notes of the B Blues Scale (B,D,E,F,F♯,A).

EX. 6

Ex. 7 is another descending riff, similar to Ex. 6. But this one resembles Rick Derringer's "Rock and Roll Hoochie Koo."

EX. 7

Ex. 8 is similar to a line Leslie West played in Mountain's "Never In My Life." The Blues Scale used this time is G♯ (G♯,B,C♯,D,D♯,F♯).

EX. 8

Ex. 9 is the first in our section of single-note riffs based on the pentatonic (five-note) scale. This riff was inspired by a line from Pink Floyd's "Money." This riff uses the notes of the D Major Pentatonic (D,E,F♯,A,B).

EX. 9

Ex. 10 is similar to "Purple Haze" by Jimi Hendrix.

EX. 10

Ex. 11 is another Hendrix-inspired riff. This one is a reflection of Jimi Hendrix's "I Don't Live Today" using a B Minor Pentatonic Scale (B,D,E,F♯,A).

EX. 11

Ex. 12 is a funky little pentatonic riff inspired by Les McCann's piano line from "Compared to What." Though this riff is made up of only a few notes, notice how the syncopated rhythm creates a good groove. Remember that rhythm is just as important as note choice when it comes to composing a classic riff.

EX. 12

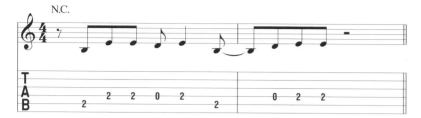

Ex. 13 is in the vein of Led Zeppelin's "Moby Dick." This riff is played with a dropped D tuning, which means the low E string is tuned a whole step down to D.

EX. 13

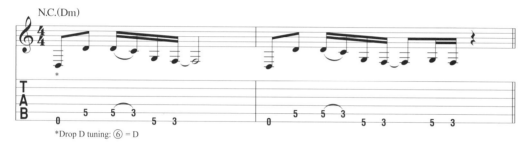

Ex. 14 is a reflection of a classic Albert King G Minor Pentatonic riff (G,B♭,C,D,F) from "Born Under a Bad Sign."

EX. 14

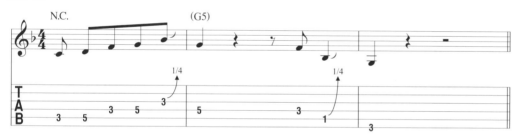

Ex. 15 is a take on Lenny Kravitz's "Are You Gonna Go My Way." This riff comes from an E Minor Pentatonic Scale (E,G,A,B,D).

EX. 15

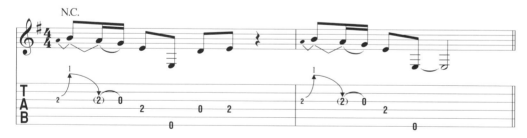

Ex. 16 is similar to a riff from "Life in the Fast Lane," by The Eagles.

EX. 16

Ex. 17 was inspired by the opening riff of Metallica's "Enter Sandman."

EX. 17

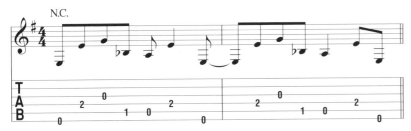

Obviously, not all single-note riffs are based on Pentatonic or Blues scales. The following riffs were based on other scales.

Ex. 18 is similar to a riff from The Offspring's "Come Out and Play."

EX. 18

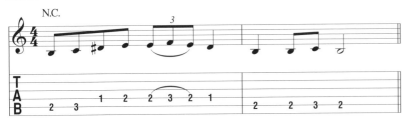

Ex. 19 is reminiscent of the G Major Scale (G,A,B,C,D,E,F#)-based riff from "Billy Jean," by Michael Jackson.

EX. 19

Ex. 20 is similar to the classic riff from Heart's "Crazy on You." This riff comes from the A Natural Minor Scale (A,B,C,D,E,F,G).

EX. 20

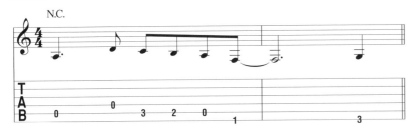

Ex. 21 is a take on a Jimi Hendrix groove riff from "Manic Depression," in 3/4.

EX. 21

Ex. 22 is similar to a riff from "Misty Mountain Hop" by Led Zeppelin. Notice how the syncopated rhythm with open strings creates a groove.

EX. 22

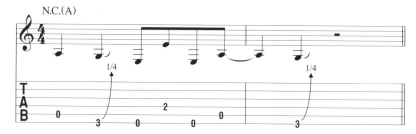

Ex. 23 has its roots in Led Zeppelin's "Immigrant Song." The riff uses only two notes an octave apart!

EX. 23

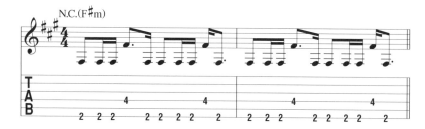

Ex. 24 reminds us of Metallica's "Jump In The Fire."

EX. 24

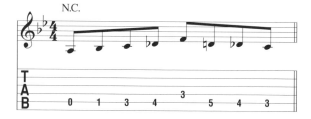

Ex. 25 is a take on a Pantera's riff from "Cowboys From Hell."

EX. 25

Ex. 26 was inspired by an Anthrax riff from "Caught in a Mosh." Note the power of the riff is created by the open string and the gradually ascending notes.

EX. 26

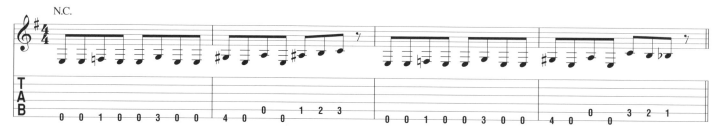

Ex. 27 is our reflection of the riff to Ozzy Osbourne's "Crazy Train." The riff consists entirely of 8th notes based on the F# Aeolian Mode (F#,G#,A,B,C#,D,E). Notice the first bar uses an F# pedal-tone, building tension.

EX. 27

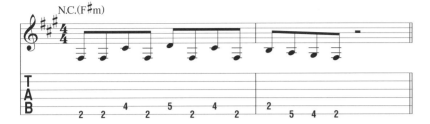

Ex. 28 is similar to a Jimi Hendrix riff from "Burning of the Midnight Lamp." The riff draws life from the C Major Scale (C,D,E,F,G,A,B). Again notice that the riff consists of only 8th notes.

EX. 28

Ex. 29 is a tough little riff inspired by Jeff Beck's version of "I Ain't Superstitious."

EX. 29

Ex. 30 is a take on David Bowie's "The Man Who Sold the World."

EX. 30

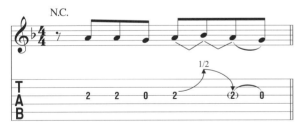

Ex. 31 relies on simplicity and its repetition throughout the song, to leave its mark. This is reminiscent of The Rolling Stones' "Satisfaction."

EX. 31

Ex. 32 has roots in the Led Zeppelin riff from "Dazed and Confused." Half-step bending is the key to making this riff speak.

EX. 32

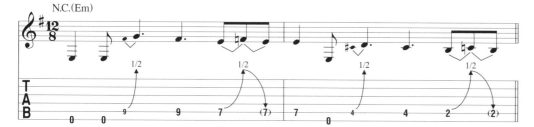

Ex. 33 was inspired by The Beatles song "I Feel Fine." Notice how the notes in the first bar outline the D7sus4 chord.

EX. 33

Ex. 34 is a reflection of the Led Zeppelin riff from "The Ocean." Notice the time signature changes in the second bar.

EX. 34

Ex. 35 is a take on Soundgarden's "Superunknown." This riff uses legato phrasing.

EX. 35

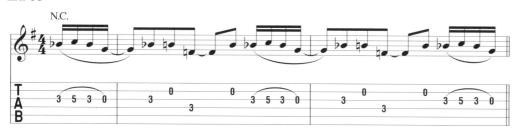

Ex. 36 is a riff arranged from a bass line that originally involves a little slapping, a little popping, and an open string bass pedal. The riff is based on The Red Hot Chili Peppers' cover of Stevie Wonder's "Higher Ground."

EX. 36

RIFFS COMBINING SINGLE NOTES WITH CHORDS

This section shows you the extension of the single-note riff, where it combines with two- or three-note chords.

Ex. 37 is in the style of Van Halen's version of The Kinks' song, "You Really Got Me."

EX. 37

Ex. 38 takes this idea even further. This riff à la Deep Purple's "Woman From Tokyo" is made up of Esus4 and E chords. Your fingers barely move.

EX. 38

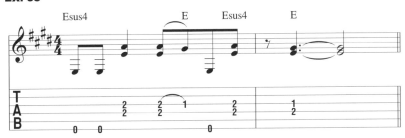

Ex. 39 is a riff based on Led Zeppelin's "Good Times Bad Times."

EX. 39

> I turned the rhythm from "Willie and the Hand Jive" into the verse.
> —Rick Derringer on "Rock and Roll Hoochie Koo"

> Three riffs that changed my life were "Over the Edge" by The Wipers, "Stone Cold Fever" from Humble Pie, but that was only for when I was a drummer. "Not Right" by The Stooges, and "Can't You Hear Me Knocking" by The Rolling Stones. After Mick Taylor left, The Stones lost it.
> —J Mascis (Dinosaur Jr.)

Ex. 40 is a riff in the style of AC/DC's "Back in Black." The chords and the single-note lines act as a call and response.

EX. 40

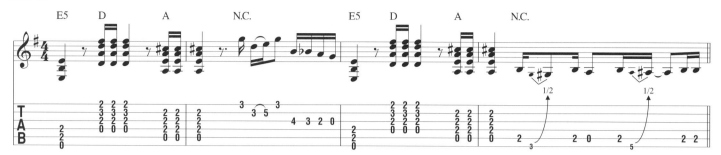

Ex. 41: Another call and response riff can be played with our interpretation of Jimi Hendrix's "Foxey Lady."

EX. 41

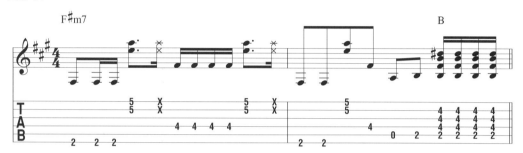

Single-note riffs are often used with the power chord, which is made up of the root note of the chord (the A of the A5 chord) and the note which is a perfect 5th away, in this case E. The next set of examples all utilize the power chords along with single-notes.

Ex. 42 is a good example of the power-chord riff. This is our take on Ted Nugent's "Cat Scratch Fever."

EX. 42

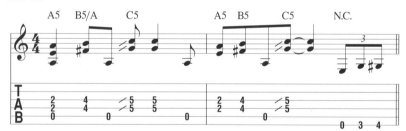

Ex. 43 is our interpretation of Neil Young's power-chord riff to "Mr. Soul." Are we the only ones who notice a resemblance to The Stones' "Satisfaction?"

EX. 43

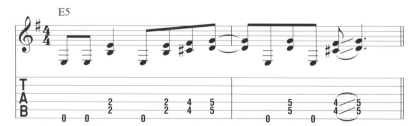

> *The first lick I can remember trying to play as a kid was "Life in the Fast Lane."*
> *I was so happy I could get it. It took me so long to get it.*
> —Ed Roland (Collective Soul)

Ex. 44 is a riff based on AC/DC's "Whole Lotta Rosie."

EX. 44

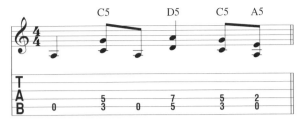

Ex. 45 is a take on Mountain's "Mississippi Queen." Here the power chords introduce the riff and the single-notes finish it.

EX. 45

Ex. 46 uses a similar idea to Ex. 45. This is a riff based on Neil Young's "Cinnamon Girl."

EX. 46

Ex. 47 is based on one of the most famous power-chord riffs of all time, Led Zeppelin's "Whole Lotta Love."

EX. 47

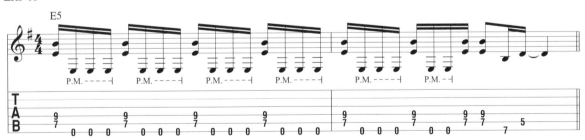

Ex. 48 is à la Metallica's "Seek and Destroy."

EX. 48

Ex. 49 is our take on "Paranoid" from Black Sabbath. Notice the use of hammer-ons.

EX. 49

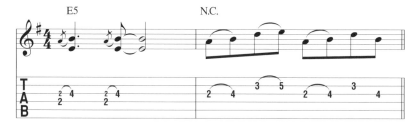

Ex. 50 is a simple riff with a lot of impact, based on The Stones' tune "Shattered."

EX. 50

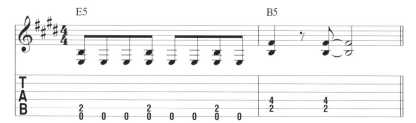

Ex. 51 is also minimal in its note choice, but powerful in its impact. This is an interpretation of riff to "Electric Head Pt. 2," by White Zombie.

EX. 51

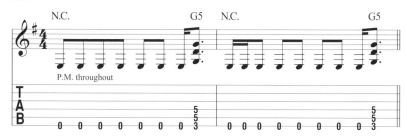

Ex. 52 is our vision of Dio's "Rainbow In The Dark."

EX. 52

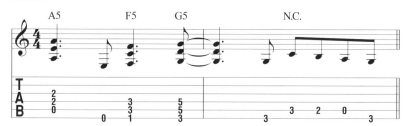

Ex. 53 is a take on "Architecture of Aggression" from Megadeth.

EX. 53

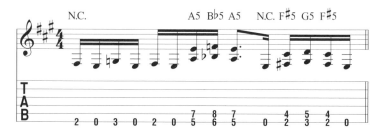

The last grouping of riffs in this section move into the more overtly melodic category.

Ex. 54 is à la the Grateful Dead's "Casey Jones."

EX. 54

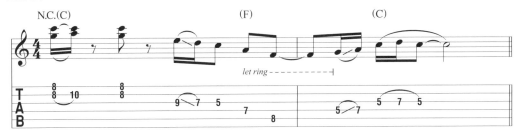

Ex. 55 is our vision of a riff from "Life's Been Good" by Joe Walsh.

EX. 55

Ex. 56 is a take on "Running from an Angel" by Hootie & the Blowfish.

EX. 56

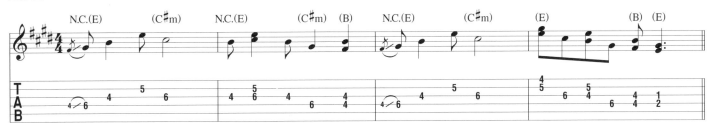

Ex. 57 is an interpretation of "Rotten Apple."

EX. 57

Ex. 58 was inspired by Eric Clapton's riff to "Layla."

EX. 58

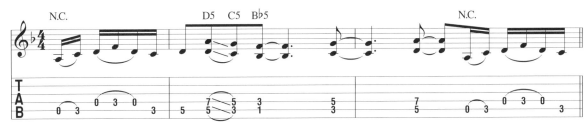

Ex. 59 is similar to Neil Young's "Hey Hey, My My." Notice how the first four notes come from the A Natural Minor Scale (A,B,C,D,E,F,G) followed by the Am chord.

EX. 59

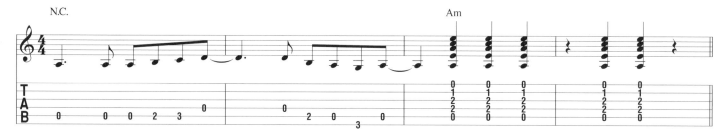

Ex. 60 is our take on Richie Valens' "La Bamba." The Beatles took this from The Isley Brothers and turned it into one of their first hits, "Twist And Shout."

EX. 60

Ex. 61 is à la "Hot for Teacher" by Van Halen. This features legato playing and slides.

EX. 61

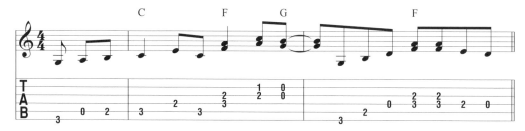

Ex. 62 reminds us of the Free song, "Mr. Big." Billy Sheehan took the title of this song to name his band.

EX. 62

> *The three riffs that changed my life are Ozzy Osbourne's "Crazy Train," "Eruption" by Van Halen, and "She" by Kiss. "Smoke on the Water" was the first one I ever did. The one out of those would definitely have to be "Crazy Train." When that first came out, the sound of that guitar and that riff was amazing.*
> —*Diamond Darrell (Pantera)*

POWER-CHORD RIFFS

In this section we are dealing strictly with power chords. The use of power chords often adds muscle and strength to the riff.

Ex.63 clearly underlines the point we just made. Here is a take on Deep Purple's "Smoke on the Water."

EX. 63

Ex. 64 is similar to the power-chord riff that brought the group Yes to the top of the charts with "Owner of a Lonely Heart."

EX. 64

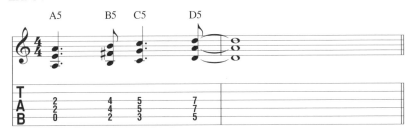

Ex. 65 is at the heart of rock 'n' roll rhythm guitar and an awful lot of blues playing as well. This is something similar to what Eric Clapton played on "I'm Tore Down."

EX. 65

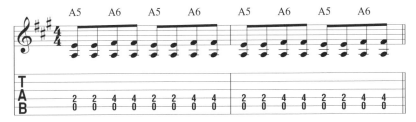

Ex. 66 is from the same vein as the previous example. This time we've interpreted The Eagles' "Already Gone."

EX. 66

Ex. 67 is our rendition of "More Human Than Human" by White Zombie. This rhythm riff is built on one chord—E5!

EX. 67

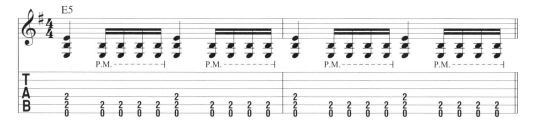

Ex. 68 reminds us of "This Is a Call" from Foo Fighters. The simplicity of this riff does not diminish its impact.

EX. 68

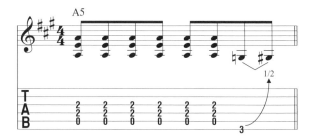

Ex. 69 is similar to "All Day and All of the Night" by The Kinks.

EX. 69

Ex. 70 is an interpretation of "Iron Man" by Black Sabbath.

EX. 70

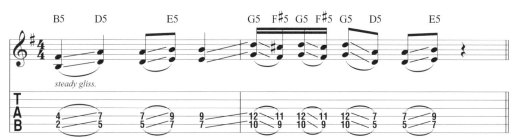

"I'm A Man" by The Yardbirds is as classic as the original (Muddy Waters). It's what they did with a simple riff to make it more of a song. It's another case of taking it to the limits. It's just a cool guitar move that builds up with the bass.
—Joe Perry (Aerosmith)

Ex. 71 is similar to a rhythm riff from "Welcome to the Jungle" by Guns N' Roses.

EX. 71

Ex. 72 reminds us of "Rock You Like A Hurricane" by the Scorpions.

EX. 72

Ex. 73 was inspired by a riff from "Quiet" by The Smashing Pumpkins.

EX. 73

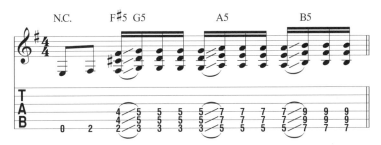

Ex. 74 is our take on how Blue Oyster Cult used rhythm riffs in "Godzilla."

EX. 74

> *I can honestly say "Maggie May" changed my life. "Ziggy Stardust" is another, and so is "Suffragette City." I would say "Honky Tonk Woman" is one of the best guitar riffs.*
>
> —Gilby Clarke (Guns N' Roses)

Ex. 75 is similar to what Bush played in their song "Everything Zen."

EX. 75

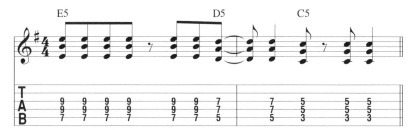

Ex. 76 is à la "Jailbreak" by Thin Lizzy.

EX. 76

Ex. 77 is a take on a rhythm riff from "Sweating Bullets" by Megadeth.

EX. 77

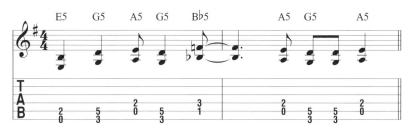

Three riffs that changed your life? Everybody is going to say "Smoke on the Water" and I'm going to say that too. I remember that coming in on the car radio when I was a little kid. I remember that so vividly. It was so powerful. I never remembered the rest of the song. All I remembered was that riff. "Sunshine of Your Love" was powerful in its own way, but it wasn't as powerful as "Smoke on the Water." It was more of a fun thing that you could hum all day. The intro to "Roll Over Beethoven" needs to be first. ELO's version blew me away. Once I first started playing, I used to sit in music stores and play that riff over and over. My first showoff song was "Day Tripper." I had it down because I figured if you played it really close to the bridge, it gets that same twang they have.
—Alex Skolnick (Testament)

CHORD-STRUMMING RIFFS

Power chords riffs punch at you. They are meant to snap your head back. Strumming riffs roll into the body. Because the chords are made up of more than just the root and 5th, they push you back with weight as well as power. To understand this, listen to any song by The Who, or, better yet, play the following examples.

Ex. 78 is à la "Substitute" by The Who.

EX. 78

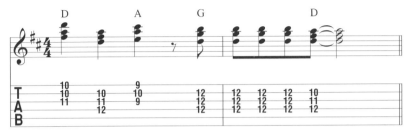

Ex. 79 is another example of how to write a hook with just three chords. This is similar to Jimi Hendrix's rendition of "Wild Thing."

EX. 79

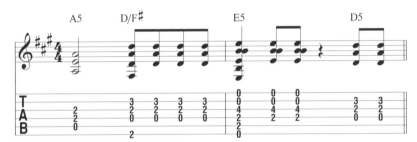

Ex. 80, à la the Clash's "Should I Stay or Should I Go," shows that you can write a memorable riff with just two chords.

EX. 80

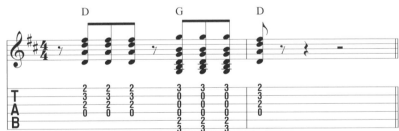

Ex. 81 breaks it down even further. The difference between the two chords in this Santana-like riff from "Oye Como Va" is essentially one note!

EX. 81

Ex. 82 is a classic case of what you can do with one note. Here is a riff where the suspended chord is resolving to a triad, à la The Who's "Pinball Wizard."

EX. 82

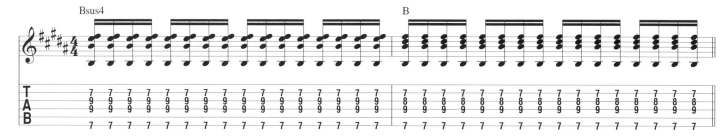

Ex. 83 is another example of suspended chords resolving to triads. This time we interpreted "Nothing Left" by Dokken.

EX. 83

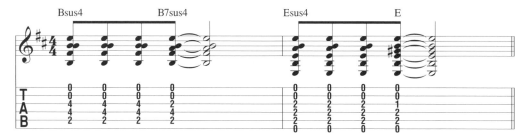

Ex. 84 is a bit of contemporary strumming that reminds us of Def Leppard's "Photograph."

EX. 84

Ex. 85 is our rendition of what Rush has done with two chords in the tune "The Spirit of Radio."

EX. 85

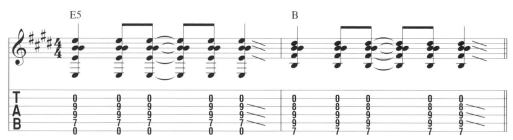

Ex. 86 is another two-chord riff. It's our take on The Doobie Brothers' "Rockin' Down the Highway." Notice the use of rests, which creates a sparse rhythm.

EX. 86

Ex. 87 is a Hendrix-inspired rendition of "Purple Haze."

EX. 87

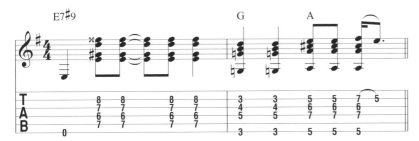

Ex. 88 is built around hammer-ons. It's similar to the James Gang piece, "Funk 49."

EX. 88

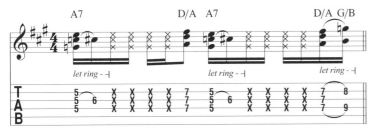

Ex. 89 is inspired by Van Halen's "Runnin' with the Devil." It too is a hammer-on based riff.

EX. 89

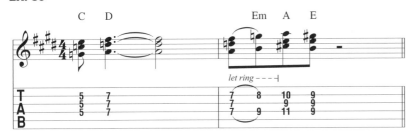

Ex. 90 is a Dire Straits-like run from "Sultans Of Swing."

EX. 90

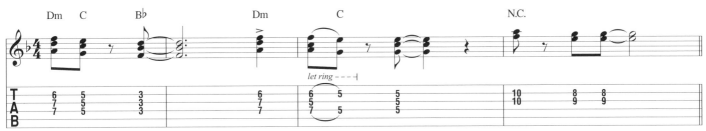

Ex. 91 is similar to what Jimi Hendrix played on "Wait Till Tomorrow."

EX. 91

Ex. 92 is a staccato riff arranged from the keyboard of Van Halen's "Jump."

EX. 92

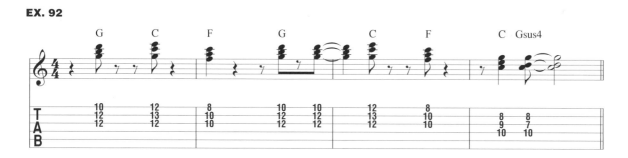

Riffs like Ex. 93, a take on Nirvana's "Smells Like Teen Spirit," helped establish alternative music in the '90s.

EX. 93

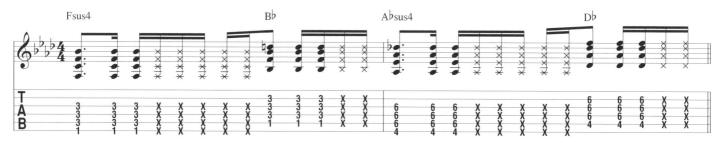

Ex. 94 resembles a Rush riff from "Free Will."

EX. 94

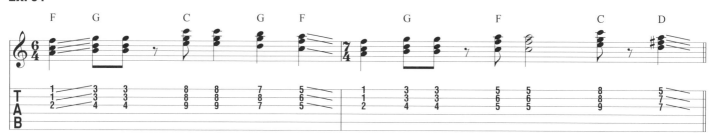

> *Of the riffs that changed my life, I remember trying to play the line in "YYZ" by Rush. I was into Black Sabbath as a little kid. I remember trying to play "Paranoid." I remember trying to get that Van Halen sound from "Ain't Talkin' About Love." Nobody could ever get that sound.*
>
> —John Petrucci (Dream Theater)

ARPEGGIO RIFFS

Arpeggio riffs are played by holding a chord and playing one note after another in sequence, each note sounding separately. This is a time honored idea that has practitioners from The Beatles to The Foo Fighters. Some people play arpeggios with fingers, others with a pick. The choice is yours. For more detail on arpeggios, check out the chapter on Acoustic Rock for Guitar.

Ex. 95 is similar to a Rush line from "Tom Sawyer."

EX. 95

Ex. 96 reminds us of "Cinnamon Girl" by Neil Young.

EX. 96

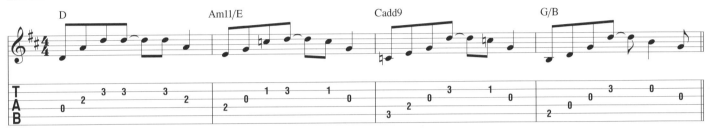

Ex. 97 is à la "Ticket to Ride" by The Beatles.

EX. 97

Ex. 98 is reminiscent of a riff from "This is a Call" by Foo Fighters.

EX. 98

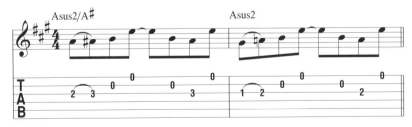

Ex. 99 reminds us of a line from "Black Hole Sun" by Soundgarden.

EX. 99

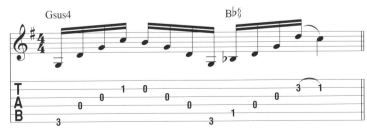

Ex. 100 is similar to "Hey You" by Pink Floyd.

EX. 100

Ex. 101 is à la "Foreclosure of a Dream" by Megadeth.

EX. 101

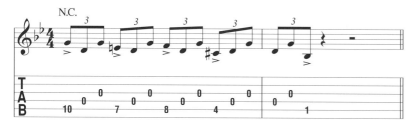

Ex. 102 reminds us of a line from "Red Barchetta" by Rush.

EX. 102

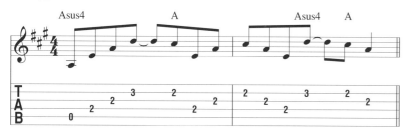

Ex. 103 was also inspired by Rush. This is our interpretation of "Entre Nous."

EX. 103

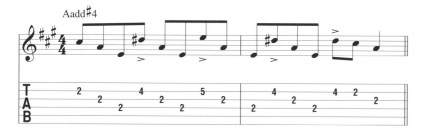

Ex. 104 sounds similar to "Fall Down" by Toad The Wet Sprocket.

EX. 104

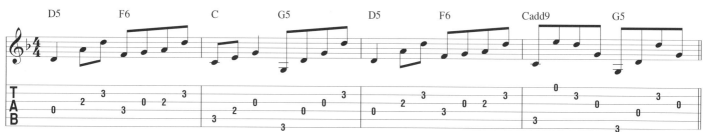

Ex. 105 is à la "Today" from The Smashing Pumpkins.

EX. 105

Ex. 106 is like "Every Breath You Take" from The Police.

EX. 106

Ex. 107 is similar to Guns N' Roses' "Sweet Child O' Mine."

EX. 107

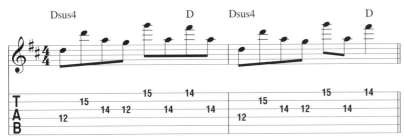

Ex. 108 is our take on The Who's "Behind Blue Eyes."

EX. 108

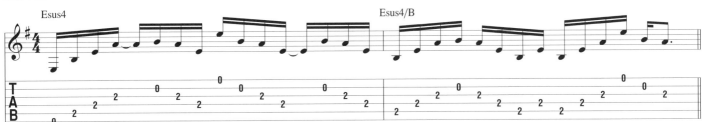

Ex. 109 is à la "Cult of Personality" from Living Colour.

EX. 109

Ex. 110 was inspired by Def Leppard's "Photograph."

EX. 110

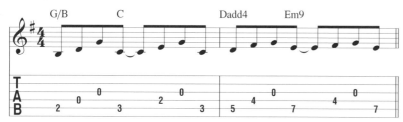

Ex. 111 is our take on Def Leppard's "Rock Rock Till You Drop."

EX. 111

Ex. 112 is a reflection on Dokken's "Nothing Left to Say."

EX. 112

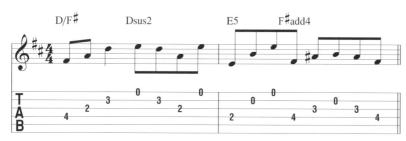

Ex. 113 is similar to "Message in a Bottle" by The Police.

EX. 113

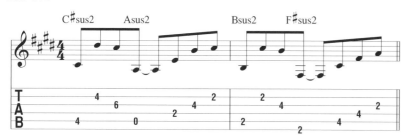

Ex. 114 is our take on Bon Jovi's "Wanted: Dead Or Alive."

EX. 114

Three riffs that changed my life were the organ riff from "Green Onions," Scotty Moore on "Mystery Train," and the solo James Burton took on "Hello Mary Lou."
—Dave Edmunds

For me it's the power-chord riff to "I've Been Waiting for You" by Nell Young, the opening riff to "Mississippi Queen" by Mountain, and the opening instrumental part in Lou Reed's "Sweet Jane" played by Dick Wagner and Steve Hunter.
—Reeves Gabrels (David Bowie)

"I Was Made to Love Her" by Stevie Wonder with James Jamerson on bass, "Thank You (Falettinme Be Mice Elf Agin)" by Sly and the Family Stone, and "Brave And Strong" by Sly and the Family Stone with Sly on bass.
—Bootsy Colllns

I liked the Isley Brothers' "Summer Breeze." That changed me. There is Chuck Berry's ever-popular clichéd intro to "Johnny B. Goode." I wore that out. Then there is B.B. King's "The Thrill is Gone."
—Ernie C (Body Count)

Three riffs that changed my life were "Purple Haze" definitely, "Whole Lotta Love," and a fast song by Al DiMeola called "Race With the Devil on Spanish Highway." My first showoff songs were "Mississippi Queen" and "Aqualung."
—Michael Wilton (Queensrÿche)

Three riffs that changed my life are the opening riff to "Whole Lotta Love," the opening riff to "Taxman," and "Breathe" off of Dark Side of the Moon.
—Chris DeGarmo (Queensrÿche)

You can always pick up a guitar and bash away and think of a good idea.
—Angus Young (AC/DC)

RECOMMENDED LISTENING

The following is a list of recordings where many riff-heavy songs reside:

American Beauty — The Grateful Dead
Anthology 2 — The Beatles
Appetite for Destruction — Guns N' Roses
Are You Experienced — The Jimi Hendrix Experience
Back in Black — AC/DC
Badmotorfinger — Soundgarden
Benefit — Jethro Tull
Boston — Boston
Brothers and Sisters — The Allman Brothers Band
Climbing — Mountain
Cowboys from Hell — Pantera
Crossroads — Eric Clapton
Decade — Neil Young
Diary of a Madman — Ozzy Osbourne
Dirt — Alice in Chains
Hotel California — The Eagles
Kiss Alive II — Kiss
Led Zeppelin II — Led Zeppelin
Machine Head — Deep Purple
Master of Puppets — Metallica
Orleans — Orleans
Paranoid — Black Sabbath
Permanent Waves — Rush
Queen II — Queen
Ten — Pearl Jam
Texas Flood — Stevie Ray Vaughan
The Joshua Tree — U2
The Police Live — The Police
Time is Tight — Booker T & the M.G.'s
Toys in the Attic — Aerosmith
Truth — Jeff Beck Group
Van Halen — Van Halen
Wheels of Fire — Cream
Who's Next — The Who

Warm-Up Exercises
FOR GUITAR

INTRODUCTION

Playing the guitar is probably no less violent than playing football. Both demand talent, skill, strength, speed, agility, and contact. And in order to play, once the music or the ball is in motion, all hands have to work together to make it happen. There is pushing and hitting, abrupt stops, and lightning fast changes of direction. Neither is something you can do well if you're not in shape for it. And one of the worst things you can do in either case is play full-on without warming up. Do that and you're bound to get hurt. Maybe not today, but somewhere down the road, playing could become painful and ultimately harmful.

To educate us on how the pros get ready before hitting the stage, we asked 11 guitarists about their warm-up routines. But to get the ball rolling—or, rather, the blood pumping—the authors offer the following observations when working with any of the exercises in the book:

We found that usually a warm-up or any finger exercise is born out of a player's effort or frustration to overcome a particular passage of a song or a difficult lick. He might invent an exercise that would help or facilitate his technique or the dexterity necessary to play those difficult parts. That's what any exercise or practice should be. It should always be related to and in consideration of the music you are trying to play. Once you get an idea from the guitarists here, invent your own warm-up exercises suitable for your own needs and the type of music you are playing.

On a nuts-and-bolts level, while Eddie Van Halen can call upon his drummer brother Alex when he needs a groove to move, the rest of us will probably call upon the trusty drum machine or a metronome. Tony MacAlpine discussed the importance of playing with a drum machine, saying, "When you practice with a drum machine or metronome, you can lock into the rhythm. It's very easy to make rhythmic mistakes. If you don't have a good understanding of what rhythmic influences are like, you'll get lost with a drum machine. With a drum machine you can fall on the beat, lay back in the groove, or be in front of the beat. The metronome is stiff. It's hard to screw that up. The metronome is a stern teacher."

A universal rule is to always start your warm-ups slowly and increase the tempo gradually. Strive for a smooth, clear, and strong execution of the exercise. Avoid sloppiness, rushing, or dragging. Keep in mind that these ideas are not only good for warm-ups, but excellent for strengthening your fingers as well.

Once you learn an exercise, look away from the music so that you can better concentrate on your own playing.

EXPLAINING TABLATURE

Tablature is a paint-by-number language telling you which notes to play on the fingerboard. Each of the six lines represents a string on the guitar. The numbers on the line indicate which frets to press down. Note that tablature does not indicate the rhythm.

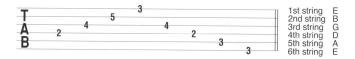

NOTATION LEGEND

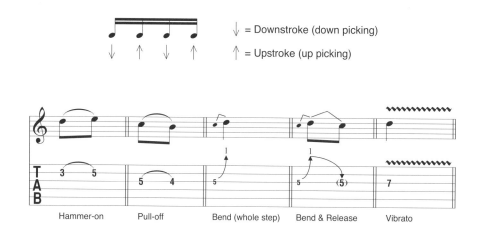

↓ = Downstroke (down picking)

↑ = Upstroke (up picking)

Hammer-on:

Pick the first (lower) note, then "hammer on" to sound the higher note with another finger by fretting it without picking.

Pull-off:

Place both fingers on the notes to be sounded. Pick the first (higher) note, then sound the lower note by "pulling off" the finger on the higher note while keeping the lower note fretted.

Bend (whole step):

Pick the note and bend up a whole step (two frets).

Bend & Release:

Pick the note and bend up a whole step, then release the bend back to the original note. All three notes are tied together; only the first note is attacked.

Vibrato:

Vibrate the note by rapidly bending and releasing the string using a left-hand finger, wrist or forearm.

Finger Number:

Suggested fingerings are included under the tab staff for all examples. However, you should experiment with different fingerings and play the one that feels most comfortable to you.

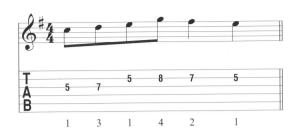

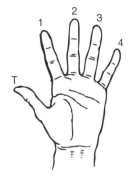

T = thumb
1 = 1st finger
2 = 2nd finger
3 = 3rd finger
4 = 4th finger

STRETCHING
with SONNY LANDRETH

"I try to impress upon people, and the younger guys especially, to get in the habit of making stretching a part of your daily routine. Tendonitis is not something that you want to deal with. It's a reality. If you are really serious and you play a lot, you practice a lot, or both, it's something that can very easily happen to anyone. I know a lot of people that have played for a long time, and they are struggling with this. It can really alter your life.

"Stretch your shoulder first, because you want to start up there. The idea is you want to warm up and loosen up the muscles before playing. And then you'll want to cool down the tendons and muscles after you get done playing.

"Now, take one arm and cross it over the other. Then take the arm facing your face and gently pull it toward you so it's stretched. You can feel it pull up into your shoulder. Do this for about 20 seconds.

"After the shoulder, I start massaging my forearm. My tendonitis is in the crook of my wrist, from the outer part of the palm, beneath the little finger. There is a tendon right there and it's inflamed all the time. I'll spend time to loosen up this area. Put your hands up, with your elbows out, just beyond your shoulders. Put your hands together so it looks like you are praying. Now slightly lift your elbows and you can feel the stretch.

"Another stretch is to have your palms face away from you. Now take one hand and place it on the other. Palm to palm, one hand is facing away from you, and the other hand is facing you. Have the hand facing you push back slightly on the hand facing away from you. Think of your fingers as one. What you are doing is getting down the forearm.

"The last thing I do is individual fingers. These are very gentle stretches. One hand presses against the other (to look like you are praying), but the fingers are separated. Press one hand against the other. Your fingers go backwards.

"Ideally, if I'm working a lot, I'll try to get going for 15 to 20 minutes first. If I'm having problems and need the full-blown affair, I'll use a moist heat first. I'll put a heating pad with moist heat on the muscles, and then start doing the stretches. Then I play for what seems like forever. At the end, when I'm done playing, I'll ice down. Especially where the prominent areas are. Ideally, the best thing to do is have a sink with ice water in it, and put your whole arm down in it, like a baseball pitcher It's like sports medicine.

"I urge people to do this because tendonitis is debilitating."

> There are things that twist my tendons up that I practice over and over again. It kills me that someone like Steve Vai would say 'You mean that lick you did?' and just knock it out.
>
> —Joe Satriani

TWO-FINGER EXERCISES
with STEVE VAI

"Did you ever do those exercises where you take your 1st and 2nd finger and you go across the strings? Do that with your 1st and 2nd finger all the way up and down the neck in half steps at four different metronome speeds. Then do that with your 1st and 3rd fingers. Then do it with your 1st and 4th fingers. Then do it with your 2nd and 3rd fingers, all the way up and all the way down. Then your 2nd and 4th fingers, and then your 3rd and 4th fingers. It's a great exercise, because the 3rd and 4th fingers aren't as strong as your 1st and 2nd. Then you do it with skipping a fret. It's the same concept. You do your 1st and 3rd fingers and skip a fret, so you've got two frets between them. Try and do that with your 2nd and 3rd fingers, skipping a fret. And you have to do it just as clean as the 1st and 2nd fingers. If you can do it, believe me, your chops will be 100% improved.

"The metronome speed is up to the user You have to start really slow so you don't even make one little mistake. I don't do these anymore. God, if I had time to sit and do exercises, that would be great. When I used to do them, I used a metronome because that's all I had."

Ex. 1 is an exercise for finger combinations 1-2, 2-3 and 3-4.

EX. 1

Diagram 1

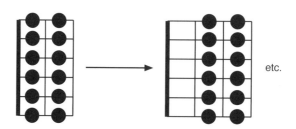

etc.

Ex. 2 is an exercise for finger combinations 1-3, 2-4, and stretching for 1-2, 2-3, 3-4.

EX. 2

Diagram 2

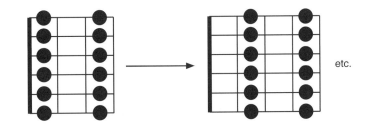

etc.

Ex. 3 is an exercise for finger combinations 1-4 and stretching for 1-3 and 2-4.

EX. 3

Diagram 3

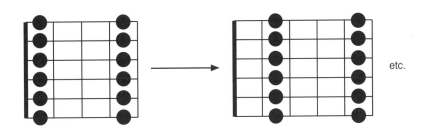

etc.

Ex. 4 is an exercise for a finger combination with stretching 1-4.

EX. 4

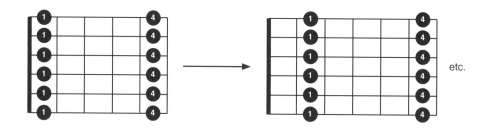

Diagram 4

BASIC THREE- AND FOUR- FINGER EXERCISES
with ROBIN TROWER

"Many years ago Robert Fripp gave me a very good warm-up exercise which I used to use. He had me use all of my fingers, starting at the bottom string, first fret. You play a note on every fret. So you go 1, 2, 3, 4 on the bottom string, and then you go up on each string from low E to high E. So you go on the E string for four frets, A string four frets and so on. After you've played the last note (G#) with your pinkie on the high E string, move up a fret and come back down the strings 4, 3, 2, 1.

"You are going up four frets, then moving up one fret, and coming back down. You start by using all of your fingers. Then what he had me do was drop one out. So you start 1, 3, 4 all the way up, move up one, and come back 4, 3, 1. Then you just do a combination of any two fingers. It was a very good exercise; no doubt about it. It gets your finger coordination going. I haven't done that one in a while, but I did do it quite religiously the year he gave it to me. He is a very good teacher."

Ex. 5 is the most basic four-finger exercise, which is good for developing equal strength in each finger.

EX. 5

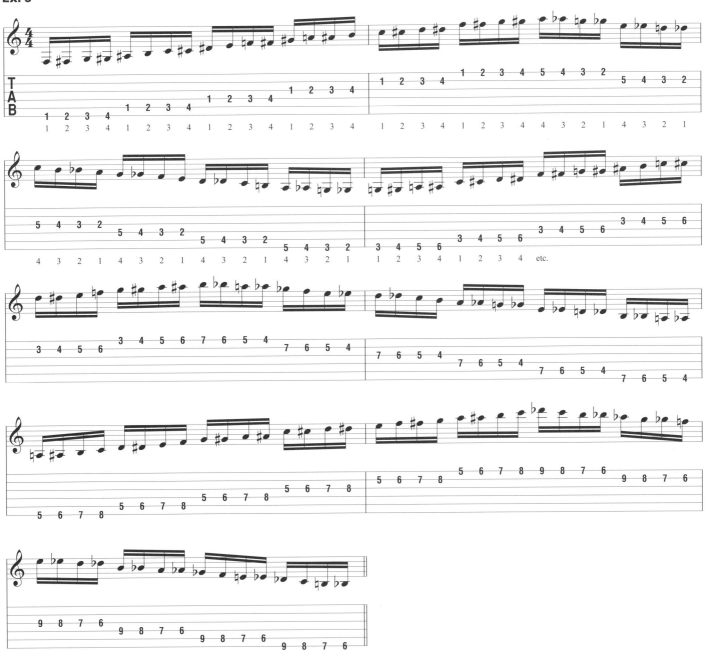

Diagram 5

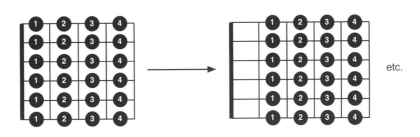

etc.

Ex. 6 shows one of the three-finger exercises. Here are some other possible combinations:

1-2-3, 1-3-2, 2-1-3, 1-2-4, 1-4-2, 2-1-4, 1-3-4, 1-4-3, 3-1-4, 2-3-4, 2-4-3, 3-2-4, 3-2-1, 2-3-1, 3-1-2, 4-2-1, 2-4-1, 4-1-2, 4-3-1, 3-4-1, 4-1-3, 4-3-2, 3-4-2, 4-2-3

Picking on Triplets

EX. 6

Diagram 6

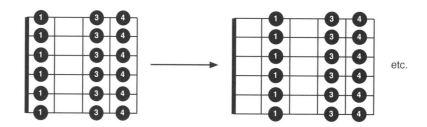

RANDOM THREE-FINGER EXERCISES AND SKIPPING STRINGS
with ROBIN TROWER

"What I do is something that Jason (Becker) showed me. It's not really an exercise, and I made it a lot simpler than what he does. Use any two strings; I take the E and A string. But you can use anything that moves the fingers very, very slowly. No need to play warm-up exercises fast. What's the point? Usually I don't have time to do anything. I just get handed the guitar and go out and play. I try and go over the first solo before I hit the stage. If I play the first solo, then it's kind of in my head a little bit. The adrenaline rush doesn't kill me. Sometimes the adrenaline is so out there at the beginning of our set that I can barely play the first solo without thinking. If it's in my head a little bit, I can go on autopilot.

"This exercise should be played all over the place, in scale, out of scale, stretched out. Just limber up."

Ex. 7 is the combination Marty described, going up the neck. Don't forget to do the same coming back down the neck as well.

EX. 7

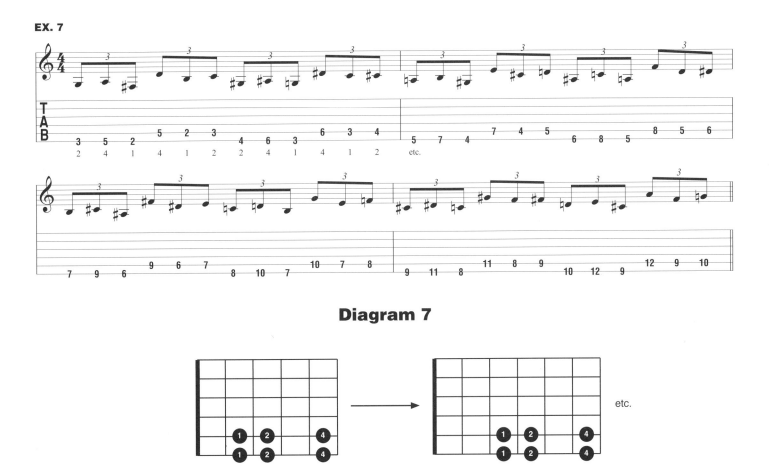

Diagram 7

Marty's exercise is a combination of 2-4-1 and 4-1-2, which are two possibilities of the many three-finger combinations that we saw in Robin Trower's exercise.

Ex. 8 is the combination going across the neck. You can go up the neck as far as you want.

EX. 8

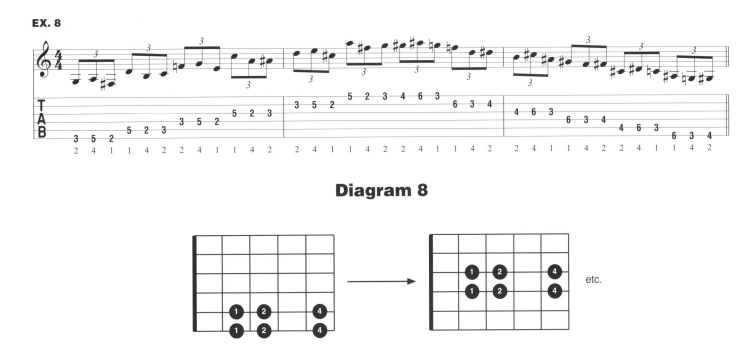

Diagram 8

Ex. 9 is the combination skipping one string going up the neck.

EX. 9

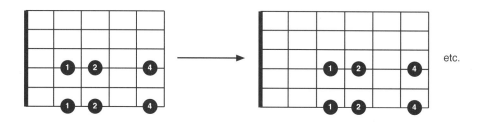

Diagram 9

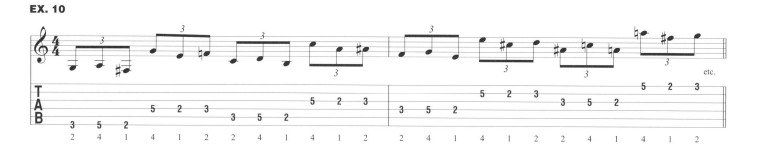

etc.

Ex. 10 is the combination skipping a string across the neck. Now experiment with other combinations of your choice in the same manner.

EX. 10

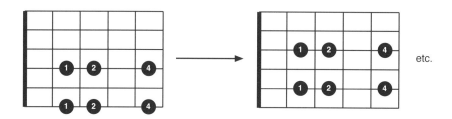

Diagram 10

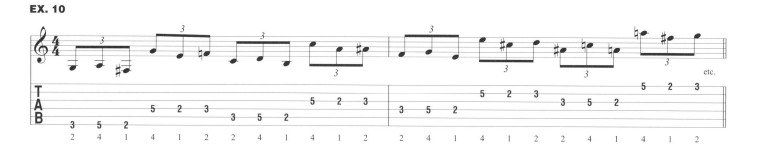

etc.

I warm up before I go on stage, but the best way to warm up for me is playing. We have a small drum kit in the dressing room, and our drummer, Mike Mangini, the king of warming up, does the sickest warm-up things. I just jam along with him. I think the best thing to do is use common sense. You start off nice and slow, whether it's a pentatonic thing or anything you choose. Play with a slow pace for a while and then sort of build it up. At the end of my warm up, Mike and I are out of control. We're playing way too many notes. But, if you warm up, you feel much better when you go on stage.

—Nuno Bettencourt

THREE-FINGER EXERCISES USING ARPEGGIOS

with PETER FRAMPTON

"I got most of my warm-up exercises from Steve Morse. I start on the A note of the low E string and play these arpeggios, moving a half step up the neck after each pattern. Sometimes I start on G. I go all the way up to the 12th fret. I do that as part of a few warm-ups that I do in the dressing room before I go on. It's good for the left hand. But do it for both hands, really, because you are using up-and-down strokes. It's just one of a few that I do that hopefully gets my coordination going and it also reminds my little finger to play."

Ex.11 is the Dom 9 arpeggio that Peter Frampton warms up with. After you get to the 12th fret, don't forget to come back down.

EX. 11

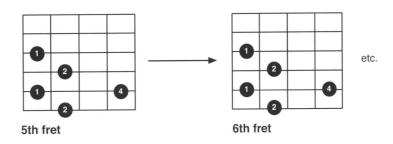

Diagram 11

5th fret   6th fret   etc.

I don't usually just sit down and practice scales. I think that is the most boring thing. It's like eating a sprout sandwich. Not for me; I need a different kind of meat. I play to records a lot. I play along with John Coltrane's 'Naima' and 'My Favorite Things,' and try to hang in there with McCoy (Tyner) and Elvin (Jones). Once the record is over, that's a good warmup exercise.

You can't play what Trane plays, so all you can do is just play the melody like he does and then just try to hang in there. When you see a hole, try to fill it like Walter Payton. When you see an opening, penetrate. That's about it. Most of the time I just put my guitar down after about 15 or 20 minutes, because when Trane and Elvin Jones take off, nobody can hang in there. Just do your best. That's the best exercise I can think of. A daily dose of Trane is the exercise that everybody should have.

—Carlos Santana

CHROMATIC SCALES AND PICKING EXERCISES
with WARREN DeMARTINI

"When I warm up, it's pretty simple. I just work on playing all downstrokes for a while, and then all upstrokes for a while, gradually mixing in to down and up. The whole thing takes about a half an hour. I'll do it till I can feel it, and then I stop and shake out. I play a chromatic scale starting with my index finger on the A note of the E string, and go chromatically up from there. Instead of going up to C# on the E, I go down to C# on the A string. So your hand only moves one fret. You play C# and D on the A string with the index finger and continue on with the rest of your fingers till you play F with the pinkie. Move down one fret and one string to the F# on the D string. Play that and G with the index finger and go up three frets with the next three fingers. Continue this pattern on the G string. When you get to the B string you go down one string, without moving back one fret. The index finger plays the E, and the pattern continues for four notes. For the high E string you go down one fret and one string to the G# on the E string. Play G# and A with the index finger and then finish the pattern all the way up to the C with your pinkie. I'll play around with this idea. Sometimes I'll do that exercise chromatically up-and-down the neck a couple of times at different speeds. For me, warming up is getting the left and right hand aligned. I learned that exercise from a friend of mine, Ron Wolfson. It's a good way to get moving. I blend downstrokes, upstrokes and combinations of the two. I found getting that loose was a good thing to do."

Ex. 12 shows the chromatic scale from the low A to high C♯ across the neck.

Picking

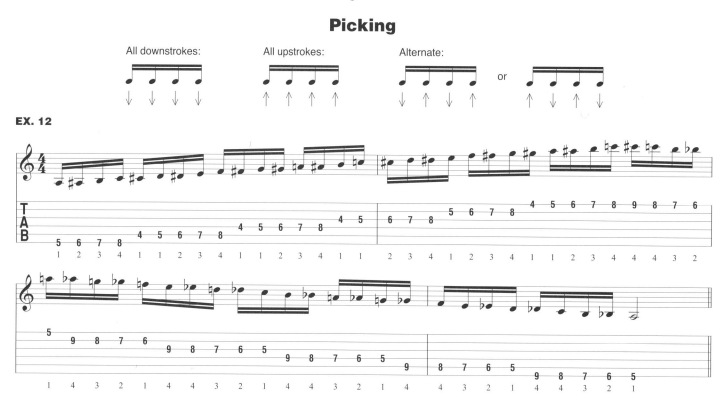

EX. 12

Diagram 12

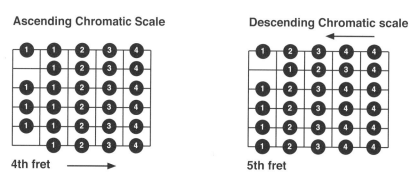

WHOLE-TONE SCALES

with ROBBIE KRIEGER

"I will just do some scales, whole-tones, half-tones, and altered scales. I'll work on a particular song that I might be having trouble with."

A whole-tone scale is a six-note scale made up entirely of whole steps. So there will be one fret between every note in the scale. Which means there are no chromatics or half steps in this scale. There are only two whole-tone scales. The second whole-note scale starts one fret away from the first one and uses the six notes which were not used in the first whole-tone scale. Having no specific key center, any note on the scale can act as a root note.

Ex. 13 is a G whole-tone scale in 2nd position: G, A, B, C♯ (D♭), D♯ (E♭), F. Watch for the stretch with the 4th finger.

EX. 13

Diagram 13
G Whole-Tone Scale

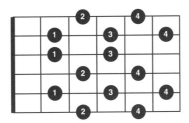

Ex. 14 is a G♯ whole-tone scale in 4th position: G♯ (A♭), A♯ (B♭), C, D, E, F♯ (G♭). Watch for the stretch with the 1st finger.

EX. 14

Diagram 14
G♯ Whole-Tone Scale

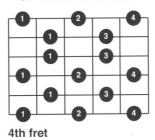

4th fret

These are but two of the many possible ways to play a whole-tone scale. Try playing it on one string, perhaps using three notes for every string. As always, make this scale and exercise your own by finding a place for it in your music.

Ex. 15 is an altered jazz scale, like Robbie mentioned. It is called a Super-Locrian or Jazz Melodic Minor Scale, up a half step from the root of a chord. Here we are presenting the G Super-Locrian (G altered scale). Notice it's exactly the same scale as A♭ Jazz Melodic Minor Scale starting from the 7th scale degree, G.

EX. 15

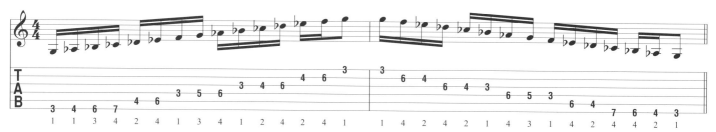

Diagram 15

G Super-Locrian (Altered) Scale

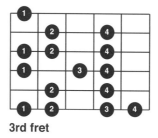

3rd fret

SCALE SEQUENCE EXERCISES
with MICHAEL WILTON

"Here is an example using a B major scale. Go up and back without a pause at the top. Start 1 note at a time, then 4s, then 3s. Remember to be legato, not staccato. Think of the mind and both hands as one."

NOTE:
1. Watch out for places where position transitions occur.
2. Remember these fingerings and the scale pattern are only suggestions; feel free to experiment.
3. Create your own sequence patterns. Practicing scales by using different sequences has been one of the most effective ways to reinforce your scale knowledge. It's not only a good test to see if you know the scale, but it also helps train your fingers and ears as well.

Ex. 16 is the B Major scale in three octaves as Michael plays it.

EX. 16

Diagram 16

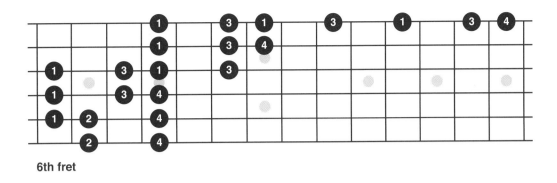

6th fret

Ex. 17 is the same scale played in a 4-group-note sequence.

EX. 17

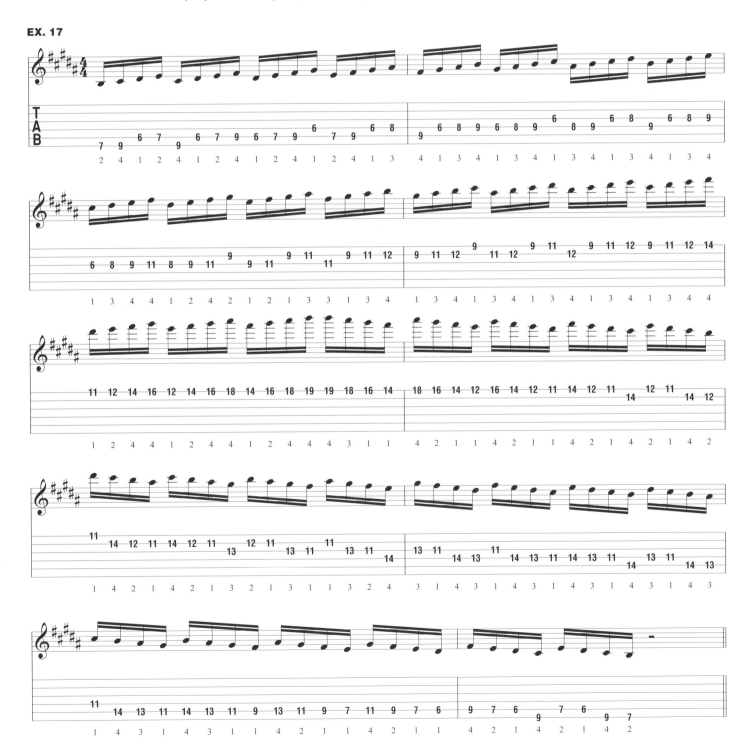

Ex. 18 is the same scale played in a 3-group-note sequence.

EX. 18

> I like to work out with a 12-string before I go on stage; play some barre chords and play some leads on 12-string. I like that a lot. It really toughens your hand up. When you go out and have a 6- string, you are ready for it. I just play blues and oldies, Beatles songs. Real bits and pieces of stuff.
>
> —Joe Walsh

PUTTING IT ALL TOGETHER
with STEVE MORSE

"One thing to do while warming up is to literally get warm. Especially if you think about your future. Everybody needs to start thinking about that if they are going to spend a lifetime playing. Think about taking care of their muscles and tendons. The first step is to develop the good habit of washing your hands in warm water. This is to get your hands warmed up and of course to get them clean. Getting your hands literally warmed up makes it easier to stretch. Then start very slowly with the easiest exercise that seems to do any good. That's doing triplets. That's going 1, 2, 3, 1, 2, 3 across each string, using three fingers. I do different patterns on each position and move up a fret each time. I start on the low E string, F note and play F, F#, G, then Bb, B, C on the A string and D#, E, F on the D and so on, going up the strings and then back down. Stay in first position and then use fingers 2, 3 and 4 to play the same notes, starting on F# and going up and down the strings. Then move to the third position and use fingers 1, 3, and 4 to do major and minor scales with three-notes-per-string, repeating a note on the G string that you will play on the B string, or playing a flat 5. It's almost a pentatonic pattern except three notes a string. You can play a minor or major pentatonic pattern three notes a string. I try to make it different each time I move up a fret, just so I don't do it too mindlessly. You have to think a little bit. The advantage of doing it this particular way is your pick changes direction every string. You get an alternate picking exercise and you don't have to worry about starting in one direction, finishing the exercise, and then starting it again in the opposite direction. Every other time you've got a new direction. In the 4th position, I might do an E Mixolydian pattern starting in 4th position starting on G#, A, B, C#, D, E, F#, G#, A, B, C#, D first finger on the B string E, F#, G#, G# again on the fourth position with your first finger A, B and then come back down. In 5th position I might do A diminished. A, B, C, D, D#, F, F#, G#, A, B, C, D, D#, F, F#, G#, A, B, slide it up one fret and then use the same scale coming down, starting with the fourth finger of the high E string with the C, B, and A, and come back down. The next one would be G# with the fourth finger. Go up and down the same scale. You can shift that last note and kind of add an extra note, rather then repeating the last note."

Ex. 19 is the chromatic 1, 2, 3 and 2, 3, 4 exercises, followed by G Natural Minor or Aeolian (or B♭ Major scale), followed by E Mixolydian (or A Major scale) and finished up with A Diminished scale, moving up one fret each time.

EX. 19

Diagram 19

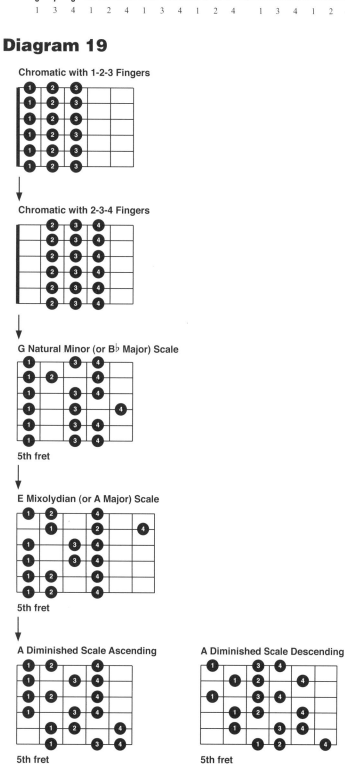

Chromatic with 1-2-3 Fingers

Chromatic with 2-3-4 Fingers

G Natural Minor (or B♭ Major) Scale

5th fret

E Mixolydian (or A Major) Scale

5th fret

A Diminished Scale Ascending

5th fret

A Diminished Scale Descending

5th fret

JAMMING SONGS AND MENTAL INFLUENCES
with RICHIE SAMBORA

"Scales were never anything to interest me as far as a warm-up exercise, before a gig, or almost any other time. I tried to get into them, but they never hit me. I always had to play songs and wrench emotion out of them. That's the way I warmed up. I start getting deep for a half hour or so before I go on, and then can go out there and feel confident that I've got the instrument in my realm. But I don't play Bon Jovi songs to warm up; I leave the spontaneity for that on stage. I just jam and get into my own grooves. A lot of them are funk oriented, blues oriented, or just kind of out there. I'm by myself and I just start playing. Sometimes I get into different influences. If you want to practice your soaring bends you play David Gilmour stuff. 'Comfortably Numb' is a wonderful solo. If you want to practice your funk playing, you play Jimi Hendrix. You get into the tune and then you can get into your head, and play around with chord changes. A lot of times I just play the tune. Nobody is going to play like Jimi anyway. I don't really take licks per say. You just let it sink in and then you move it. On the Adventures of Ford Fairlane soundtrack album I did 'The Wind Cries Mary.' At the end of the song I tried to use as many Hendrix signature riffs as I could. I put them in that key and mess with them orchestrally, actually. If you want to practice your blues playing, you start playing Eric Clapton, Johnny Winter, B.B. King, or whatever you are going to go for. Get your vibrato cooking. As far as songs and changes go, anything off Layla or by Cream. Then you get into Zeppelin, and you get rolling. Your mind goes off on its own and you become you. Sometimes, if I don't have enough time to warm up sufficiently I use the Grip Master. That will get you close because it works all those muscles."

NOTE:
1. While Richie warms up by jamming, we decided to take some licks he may be playing and move them up the neck in the more traditional manner of warm-up exercises. This is a good way to practice a lick you want to nail down, while improving your hand coordination and ear training.
2. Continue these exercises in the same manner further up the neck and try other string combinations.
3. Similarly, take any lick you are working on and move it up and down the neck repeatedly.

Ex. 20 is a lick taken and arranged from "Comfortably Numb," and moving up a half-step.

EX. 20

Ex. 21 is a lick from Clapton's version of "Hideaway," moving up in half steps.

EX. 21

Ex. 22 is a lick from "Stairway to Heaven," moving up in half steps.

EX. 22

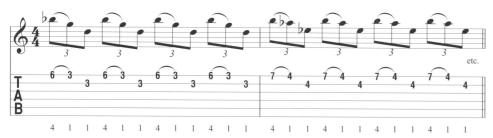

BENDING IN TUNE AND VIBRATO
with NEAL SCHON

"I don't really have a warm-up exercise that I do. I would say a good warm-up exercise for me is being in tune with my stretches and vibrato. There are so many different types of vibrato. You can sit down with a piano, a tuning fork, or someone can hum out a note to you. Then, on the G string, play the note a whole step down from the note struck on the piano, and make sure that your stretching up is in tune with that note. Again, the piano player hits the note and you stretch up to the note and hit the vibrato. Use fast vibrato, use slow vibrato, use extremely slow vibrato, and make sure that note always comes back to the top when you come off it. Practice just holding the note forever while stretching up to it. I think that is a great warm-up exercise for all new guitar players that play a million notes. Practice just hitting one note and making it sing. Try stretching it up completely in tune with whatever kind of vibrato that you chose to put on it. And leave it there. Then go up to the B string and do the same thing. Go up to the E string and do the same thing. Then go back to the B string and go back to the G string and then stretch down on the G string. Pull it. Then move to the D. The D is more difficult, because they are wound strings. Try the A string, You can do it on all of them. I do that, trying to get my voice together on the guitar. It's so important to be able to bend in tune if you want it to sing like someone like Aretha Franklin or Stevie Wonder. You've got to do those types of things."

Ex. 23 is a vibrato exercise in fifth position with the third finger moving across the neck.

NOTE:
1. When adding vibrato to a note, relax your shoulder and wrist.
2. Fully sustain each note for a whole-note value.
3. Concentrate on a stable and clear tone.
4. Try other places, other fingers, and different note values.
5. Experiment with different kinds of vibrato, such as short, wide, slow, rapid, etc.

EX. 23

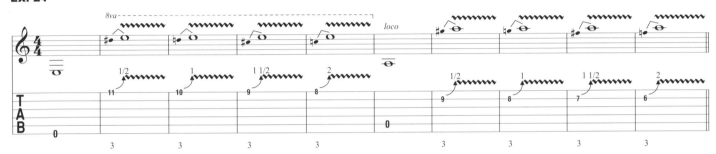

Ex. 24: Play an open E string (or Open A) and let it ring. Using the low E note (or A note) as your target, practice bending various notes on the E and B strings until they are perfectly in tune with the E or A note. Try this on other strings as well, and use Neal's suggestion to play fast, slow, or extremely slow vibrato on each note.

EX. 24

I don't like to sit down and practice for the sake of practicing. I warm up before shows, because I found that it's a necessity and I do play better during the show.

—Slash

I've never sat down and practiced. To me, there is no better way to make it boring than to sit down and do the same thing over and over again for a long time. I'll never be Steve Vai because of that, but too bad. I just like to play and make music. I play with the stereo. That's recreation to me. I can put on AC/DC's 'Back in Black' and just solo over the whole record. That's a good workout.

—Scotti Hill (Skid Row)

Get Better at Guitar

...with these Great Guitar Instruction Books from Hal Leonard!

101 GUITAR TIPS
INCLUDES TAB

STUFF ALL THE PROS KNOW AND USE

by Adam St. James

This book contains invaluable guidance on everything from scales and music theory to truss rod adjustments, proper recording studio set-ups, and much more. The book also features snippets of advice from some of the most celebrated guitarists and producers in the music business, including B.B. King, Steve Vai, Joe Satriani, Warren Haynes, Laurence Juber, Pete Anderson, Tom Dowd and others, culled from the author's hundreds of interviews.
00695737 Book/CD Pack..........................$16.95

AMAZING PHRASING
INCLUDES TAB

50 WAYS TO IMPROVE YOUR IMPROVISATIONAL SKILLS

by Tom Kolb

This book/CD pack explores all the main components necessary for crafting well-balanced rhythmic and melodic phrases. It also explains how these phrases are put together to form cohesive solos. Many styles are covered – rock, blues, jazz, fusion, country, Latin, funk and more – and all of the concepts are backed up with musical examples. The companion CD contains 89 demos for listening, and most tracks feature full-band backing.
00695583 Book/CD Pack..........................$19.95

BLUES YOU CAN USE
INCLUDES TAB

by John Ganapes

A comprehensive source designed to help guitarists develop both lead and rhythm playing. Covers: Texas, Delta, R&B, early rock and roll, gospel, blues/rock and more. Includes: 21 complete solos • chord progressions and riffs • turnarounds • moveable scales and more. CD features leads and full band backing.
00695007 Book/CD Pack..........................$19.95

FRETBOARD MASTERY
INCLUDES TAB

by Troy Stetina

Untangle the mysterious regions of the guitar fretboard and unlock your potential. *Fretboard Mastery* familiarizes you with all the shapes you need to know by applying them in real musical examples, thereby reinforcing and reaffirming your newfound knowledge. The result is a much higher level of comprehension and retention.
00695331 Book/CD Pack..........................$19.95

FRETBOARD ROADMAPS – 2ND EDITION

ESSENTIAL GUITAR PATTERNS THAT ALL THE PROS KNOW AND USE

by Fred Sokolow

The updated edition of this bestseller features more songs, updated lessons, and a full audio CD! Learn to play lead and rhythm anywhere on the fretboard, in any key; play a variety of lead guitar styles; play chords and progressions anywhere on the fretboard; expand your chord vocabulary; and learn to think musically – the way the pros do.
00695941 Book/CD Pack..........................$14.95

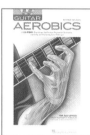

GUITAR AEROBICS
INCLUDES TAB

A 52-WEEK, ONE-LICK-PER-DAY WORKOUT PROGRAM FOR DEVELOPING, IMPROVING & MAINTAINING GUITAR TECHNIQUE

by Troy Nelson

From the former editor of *Guitar One* magazine, here is a daily dose of vitamins to keep your chops fine tuned! Musical styles include rock, blues, jazz, metal, country, and funk. Techniques taught include alternate picking, arpeggios, sweep picking, string skipping, legato, string bending, and rhythm guitar. These exercises will increase speed, and improve dexterity and pick- and fret-hand accuracy. The accompanying CD includes all 365 workout licks plus play-along grooves in every style at eight different metronome settings.
00695946 Book/CD Pack..........................$19.99

GUITAR CLUES
INCLUDES TAB

OPERATION PENTATONIC

by Greg Koch

Join renowned guitar master Greg Koch as he clues you in to a wide variety of fun and valuable pentatonic scale applications. Whether you're new to improvising or have been doing it for a while, this book/CD pack will provide loads of delicious licks and tricks that you can use right away, from volume swells and chicken pickin' to intervallic and chordal ideas. The CD includes 65 demo and play-along tracks.
00695827 Book/CD Pack..........................$19.95

INTRODUCTION TO GUITAR TONE & EFFECTS

by David M. Brewster

This book/CD pack teaches the basics of guitar tones and effects, with audio examples on CD. Readers will learn about: overdrive, distortion and fuzz • using equalizers • modulation effects • reverb and delay • multi-effect processors • and more.
00695766 Book/CD Pack..........................$14.99

PICTURE CHORD ENCYCLOPEDIA

This comprehensive guitar chord resource for all playing styles and levels features five voicings of 44 chord qualities for all twelve keys – 2,640 chords in all! For each, there is a clearly illustrated chord frame, as well as *an actual photo* of the chord being played! Includes info on basic fingering principles, open chords and barre chords, partial chords and broken-set forms, and more.
00695224..........................$19.95

SCALE CHORD RELATIONSHIPS
INCLUDES TAB

by Michael Mueller & Jeff Schroedl

This book teaches players how to determine which scales to play with which chords, so guitarists will never have to fear chord changes again! This book/CD pack explains how to: recognize keys • analyze chord progressions • use the modes • play over nondiatonic harmony • use harmonic and melodic minor scales • use symmetrical scales such as chromatic, whole-tone and diminished scales • incorporate exotic scales such as Hungarian major and Gypsy minor • and much more!
00695563 Book/CD Pack..........................$14.95

SPEED MECHANICS FOR LEAD GUITAR
INCLUDES TAB

Take your playing to the stratosphere with the most advanced lead book by this proven heavy metal author. *Speed Mechanics* is the ultimate technique book for developing the kind of speed and precision in today's explosive playing styles. Learn the fastest ways to achieve speed and control, secrets to make your practice time really count, and how to open your ears and make your musical ideas more solid and tangible. Packed with over 200 vicious exercises including Troy's scorching version of "Flight of the Bumblebee." Music and examples demonstrated on CD. 89-minute audio.
00699323 Book/CD Pack..........................$19.95

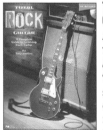

TOTAL ROCK GUITAR
INCLUDES TAB

A COMPLETE GUIDE TO LEARNING ROCK GUITAR

by Troy Stetina

This unique and comprehensive source for learning rock guitar is designed to develop both lead and rhythm playing. It covers: getting a tone that rocks • open chords, power chords and barre chords • riffs, scales and licks • string bending, strumming, palm muting, harmonics and alternate picking • all rock styles • and much more. The examples are in standard notation with chord grids and tab, and the CD includes full-band backing for all 22 songs.
00695246 Book/CD Pack..........................$19.99

1013